The
Happiness Playlist

The
Happiness
Playlist

The True Story

Of Healing My Heart

With Feel-Good Music

MARK MALLMAN

Think Piece Publishing | *Minneapolis*

ISBNs: 978-0-9863607-3-2 (paperback); 978-0-9863607-4-9 (ePub); 978-0-9863607-5-6 (Kindle)

Library of Congress Catalog Number: 2018964032
Printed in the United States of America
First Printing: 2019
23 22 21 20 19   5 4 3 2

Book designed and set in type by Mayfly Design
Front cover photo courtesy of Lauren Wuornos
Back cover photo and author photo courtesy of Wilson Webb

Think Piece Publishing
433 S. 7th St.
No. 2016
Minneapolis, MN 55415
www.thinkpiecepublishing.com

the creeping void. Such is the power of "We're Going to Be Friends" by the White Stripes. The magic of "I Wanna Dance with Somebody" by Whitney Houston or "On Melancholy Hill" by Gorillaz. The playlist becomes a newfound musical map to safe harbor. Once, I knew peace. I will stop at nothing to return there. Difficult does not mean impossible.

In a hospital emergency room I'm told the paranoia is the result of postponed grief. An amygdala hijack. The fear of fear. Mom died a year and half earlier. A part of me went with her.

"Sometimes the brain waits to process a trauma," the doctor says. "Now it's ready."

My therapist tells me to surround myself with people who lift me up. A few weeks after that, I meet Annie.

It starts over artichoke dip. When she laughs, light catches her cheekbones in slivers of two moons. She parts her hair on the right, and complains her fingers are too long. But they are the fingers of a queen alien who's been traveling the universe in search of the perfect mandarin orange. Elegant fingers as long as this summer that has come to an end. Soon, my favorite thing is to tell Annie, "I love you, too."

If I cry, which I often do, she doesn't see it as weak.

"You got this. You can do it, Mark," Annie says.

One day a Whole Foods opens two blocks away. Soon, rows of slick condos are built. The price of sandwiches goes up at the coffee shop. Gentrification pushes all the filth out, including me. I am given nine months' notice and the opportunity to stay in a refurbished version of my loft for the low price of double my rent. I'm shown a floor plan. It will be remodeled to look like the inside of a Panera Bread store.

I move to a duplex on the south side of Minneapolis. It's on Cedar Avenue, six blocks from Annie. There is one restaurant between us. We swear we'll never eat there. There is a

It's 3 a.m. I'm afraid of the dark. I'm afraid of my hands. An airplane flies over the sun and I hide under the bed. Something is wrong. I'm shaking. I'm crying. I'm having a panic attack that doesn't go away. Not in the morning. Not the day after. Not a week later. To sleep is a nightmare. To be awake is a nightmare too. How can I stop it? I give up sugar. I stop drinking. I also quit caffeine, antiperspirant, and multivitamins. Is it my laundry detergent? This shampoo? That allergy medication? I throw it all in the garbage. Nothing changes. I'm frightened to drive. I'm frightened to open doors. I'm frightened to be alive. The panic attack lasts two months.

A converted Lee jeans factory sits next to a freeway ramp in downtown Minneapolis. It is run down with urban decay. The floors are warped. The bathroom is a utility shower. There is no quiet. No sleep. No such thing as calm in the city. I live here.

Music is my only escape. Not all music. My favorite artists have become terrifying. Radiohead, Joy Division, and Patti Smith are ridden with bleak lyrics and ghostly overtones. Classic musicals calm me. "Singin' in the Rain," "Love Me Tender," and "My Fair Lady" bring calm. My heart rate slows a bit. Breathing comes easier. I used to scoff at what now is saving me: happy endings. When the musical is over, the fear returns.

The Happiness Playlist is created. It grows from a Bob Marley song repeating on headphones. "One Love." This has never been a favorite song, but it's a welcomed joy against

Foreword

The first time I met Mark Mallman, I was looking at tigers at the Minnesota Zoo. Mark seemed so nice that I assumed he was making fun of me. The second time I met him was when we performed together at First Avenue: I was reading from a book I'd written titled *Killing Yourself to Live*, while Mark would periodically interject live musical interludes inspired by musicians who had died young. As one might expect, it's hard to compete against the energy of a rock frontman when all you have to offer the audience are ironic passages from a memoir. Mark blew me off the stage. But you know, that was one instance where it was really an honor to be obliterated in public. There are so many artists (musical or otherwise) who want to present themselves as *creative*, which usually just means they can't hold a job and want people to give them credit for being vaguely annoying. Mark is the exception to this cliché. He is legitimately original, exclusively motivated by a desire to conquer the strange obstructions he builds inside his mind. He's talented, sincere, singular, and weird. And he's hyper-competitive, but only against himself.

—Chuck Klosterman

You're not a true bachelor until you use a slice of bread as a napkin.

On a stack of dictionaries sits Maneki-Neko, my fortune cat. Anything smiling and waving is welcome. Such are the methods of design therapy, to cram as much happy crap into the house as possible.

On the fridge are pictures of Gilligan, a drawing of Saint Francis, my nephews, a handout from the doctor's office that lists "Fifty Ways to Take a Break," and a picture of a Zen center I've never visited. A handwritten message reads "Have a good day. Buy a hot dog. Love, Dad."

There is also a laminated photo of Mom. She wears a white lace dress. A green and lavender corsage is pinned above her heart. Her hair curls in loose, gold ringlets. It was taken the day of my brother's wedding. Mom's smile is off center and true. In her obituary, it says, "She was the embodiment of joy."

The bedroom is white and sparse. Over the blinds hang floor-length lace curtains. They diffuse the light when the sun rises though the east window. Then the room becomes a grapefruit, bright and on fire. A fan stays on to cover up ear ringing. On a hook on the door hangs a Minnesota Twins ballcap from one of two performances I've given during games. The cap makes me proud to get out of bed and hustle another musical day.

The three-tiered bookshelf hosts titles like *The Stainless Steel Rat Saves the World*, *College for Sinners*, *Warlord of Kor*, and the screenplay to *Grease*. The bottom shelf is crammed with a multitude of unread self-help books. The middle shelf holds *The Martian Chronicles*, *Jonathan Livingston Seagull*, a gifted copy of *Harry Potter* that folds over at the first page, the autobiography of Jenna Jameson, and *Peter Pan*.

To say I own a Picasso isn't a lie. On the south wall hangs

October

If a person asks me about my home, I say, "It's the opposite of a hospice." In a Dollar Store plastic frame hangs an 8x11 computer printout reading "Think positive and positive things will happen." The windows stay open as much as possible. My bowling ball waits by the front door for fighting off robbers. Rent goes out on time. My plants are both named Robert. They are going on two years old. It's the longest I've kept anything alive.

The bathroom is lime green. Above my toilet is a sign that says "Do what makes you happy." I own enough hairspray to get me into an outpatient program. The medicine cabinet holds no medicine. Sometimes I take cold showers. A study shows they induce calm in test subjects. If anything makes a person feel like a test subject, it's a cold shower.

The checkerboard tile in my kitchen gets filthy quick, especially in winter when dirty snow tracks in. Dad's advice is to wash only the white ones.

On a dry-erase board is a list of things to do: *Quiet the mind. Breathe/Love. Gym. Nature. Kindness. Water—Health. Sunshine. People + Joy.* I've never erased it.

In regard to cooking, the fire alarm urges me to order out. Everything else is microwaved. Once I microwaved salmon.

and mathematics. You meet at a bus stop. You meet at a bar. Movies are wrong; nobody ever meets in aquariums. It's a numbers game of readiness and mutual desire. A hungry crocodile, spewed from a cyclone, that bites you in the head, even though you'd been hiding at a safe distance. You try to write just one love song, but the components can't be distilled. The depth can't be measured. This is why nobody knows how deep in love they are until it's over.

After a beautiful year together, something's missing. It's glacial. We break up. No hard feelings. We agree to stay close. We still go to the grocery and to the mall, watch movies with Gilligan under a blanket, and still say, "I love you."

After the movie, I drive the six blocks back to my place and message her.

"I had a fun day together."

"Me, too."

"Also, I feel lost inside. I'm sorry."

"Don't be sorry. So do I."

Then I text but never send, "Annie, don't go. I love you. Please stay." We've had that conversation before. She doesn't like repeating unproductive things that never lead anywhere healthy. I delete it and sleep alone in my room. She's right.

cemetery between us. We swear we'll never eat there either. It looks peaceful inside but we only make jokes about it.

"Annie, if you were a ghost, where would you choose to haunt?"

"I guess I'd hang out in a theater and watch movies all the time."

"The same movie five times a day?"

"No, in a megaplex where there's more than one movie. Oooooh, I got one! How about a ghost who is haunting another ghost?"

"A meta haunting. Brilliant."

When Annie is excited, she makes up songs. "Driving! Driving! Driving to the zoooooo!" is a favorite of mine. When she is sad, she vanishes into the couch with her dog, Gilligan, a rescue, a Kentucky stray. He is a Boston terrier mix. Annie says he's part pug. I say he's part pit bull. Dad calls him Fatso. One of us is correct.

Annie and I share a love of animals. How they clean and protect each other. How they press their heads into soft spots and sleep. When she goes on work trips, the dog stays with me. I give him spoons of peanut butter, let him sleep on my bed, and call him Mr. Boodles.

On account of his runaway past, Gilligan is easily frightened. He doesn't talk about it. Whatever he saw in Louisville is something he'd prefer to forget.

In storms, Gilligan squeezes between the bathtub and the sink. No matter how many times you tell him he is safe, he can't be convinced.

For my birthday, Annie makes me a terrarium in a fish bowl with a rubber ant and bee hanging out together on a rock. "That's us!"

When I get it home, I cry.

From what I can tell, love results from timing, chaos,

my prized Picasso (poster), *Three Musicians*. A $10 Picasso poster is a Picasso nonetheless. Aside from three musicians, there's a dog in the painting. Therefore, the title is flawed. Hadn't Picasso heard a dog howl to a clarinet? Hadn't he listened to one whine with an accordion? A terrible dog musician is a musician nonetheless. The painting/poster should be titled "Four Musicians: One Is a Dog."

Some crystals rest on the nightstand: amethyst for dreams, rose quartz for love, black tourmaline to protect against evil, and some polished stone to prevent worrying. These crystals are the most expensive things on my nightstand, but not the most valuable. A ceramic angel stands five inches tall. She has wire wings, brown hair in a pony tail, and no face. Her hands are apart, but praying. If she wasn't an angel, I'd assume she was clapping. The little sculpture is from a collection of angels Mom kept on her dresser. Dad brought it for me. On the bottom are printed the words "Angel of Happiness."

Some nights, a valve opens in the back of my neck. Fear crawls on my body like spiders. A chilling chemical leaks into my spine. I grasp the angel in my hand, or sometimes to my forehead. With deep breaths, calm builds in soft surges.

Dad and I talk on the phone twice a day.

"I'm having anxiety," I say.

"Think of where you were last year or the year before. You've been doing a good job. It'll pass."

"I worry I'm sick. I worry I'm dying." I pull the covers off my head. "I don't want to be sick. I don't want to die."

"It's good you don't want to die, Mark. That's a good thing. Also, we don't have much say in the matter."

"You make a strong argument. OK, I won't die."

"Thanks, me either. Try to relax. Get some fresh air. Get out of the house."

"I love you, Dad."

"I love you, too."

We hang up. My worry is overwhelming. I worry about my blood pressure. I worry about my liver. I worry about politics, climate change, the animals in factory farms, and nuclear war. I worry that the hair dye I use is seeping through my skull. This slows me down, but it can't stop me from living in my heart. I'm not going to let worry eat my time. I will fight.

A memory comes. On his one-year birthday, my nephew stood, wobbling in a circle of singing adults. He grinned so big his cheeks forced the eyes closed. Love radiated and reflected back. Music was responsible. This raises a hypothesis. Will a steady diet of positive music keep me from the muck of sadness? An experiment is begun. I decide to listen exclusively to The Happiness Playlist. The length of the experiment is undetermined. If it works, maybe forever.

I go out dancing. My evening shoes have gold laces. Two necklaces clipped together dangle low on my torn shirt. I wear red camouflage pants and my denim vest. It has spikes on the collar. The word PARASITE is airbrushed in all caps on back. My hair is moussed and locked with an anti-frizz 48-hour hold. If it can't be said with hair, it can't be said.

It's drizzling, always on the windshield but never in the air. Streetlights flicker. In Minneapolis, rain is just warm snow. It seeps through clothes till a person is raining on the insides. I listen to "Rapper's Delight" by the Sugarhill Gang and drive to the club.

Minneapolis. Mary Tyler Moore never lived here. She never got chased off Hidden Beach for skinny-dipping. She never staggered from the CC Club or passed out on the First Avenue dance floor. She never saw the cockroaches on an unnamed diner's wall or had a chef throw a plate at her across the kitchen. She never puked in the stairwell of the old Dayton's ramp. She never finished a Wondrous Punch from the Red Dragon or sang "Bootylicious" to a room of strangers at the Vegas Lounge. She never lived here. She never grieved here. Yet she's the one with a bronze statue on Nicollet Mall. The nightclub is called Icehouse. Inside, Maurice reclines on the bar. He is tapping a beer bottle to the rhythm of the music. Maurice has toured the world many times. Anything around him becomes a drum. Stage walls. Booze bottles. Cats. He is a drummer/rapper that grew up outside of Milwaukee too. He wears his beard trimmed short and a blaze orange trucker cap that reads "Twerk." His eyebrows are thick and expressive when he speaks. Aside from music, he has an outstanding ability for arguing.

Maurice isn't sold on the idea of a Happiness Playlist. To him, drowning yourself in one emotion is denial.

"You're deluding yourself, Mallman."

"No, I just can't be a nihilist anymore," I say. "Look at Cobain. Dude didn't write a single happy song and what happened?"

"Karma," he says, knocking back half his beer in one gulp.

"That's a bad example. My point is songs can be self-fulfilling prophecies. I can't afford gloom for gloom's sake right now. "

"Then why not write about magic?"

"Magic? I don't see the connection."

"The magic of music. There's this guy online, Alan Moore is his name. He wears lots of rings. Looks like Gandalf the Grey. He's so serious about magic that he's got a landline."

"What does a landline have to do with magic?"

"It's about living off the grid."

"A landline is still on the grid."

"But less on the grid."

On the dance floor are sounds of rubber bands and aircraft carriers. Waveforms of euphoria. Fists pump. Shiny purple backpacks sling low. Bare muscles are laid out for all to see. People have hundreds of bracelets on one arm, rail vodka soda in one hand, and a cellphone in the other. Tongues stick out for selfies. They are interracial, intertwined, and intergalactic. Glorious and free.

Maurice and I watch three of our musical associates slip into the bathroom. He flares his nostrils and sniffs.

"Eh," I shrug my shoulders. "I'm only here to dance."

I hit the floor. Disco beams reduce us to rainbow silhouettes. We are radiant beings in spiked bracelets, wet with sweat. A woman flips backward to the floor on her bare knees. She wears a charcoal and green screen print of the universe. Once the beat drops, we all scream along. I am washed over in a scandal of instinct and desire.

The Big Bang was the first music. It was a drum solo. Then came cave noise, primal beats of rocks and bones. Blood songs. Songs of birth, sex, and death. Songs that bend reality. Is God music?

At bar close, I edge my way through the crowd to the door. A woman in a sheer black blouse with sequin pineapples over her breasts locks eyes with a stranger. Three friends lean together and raise their middle fingers for a picture. They are all wearing tropical shirts. My ears buzz a ring modulation.

That night I fall asleep listening to "Fantasy" by Mariah Carey. My sleep unfolds in abstract waves. Scary monsters. Grief dreams. I wake up several times. The horror lingers but not the story. I don't remember the dreams, just the fear. None of this has to do with Mariah. She's innocent in the case of my nightmares.

In the morning, my eyelashes are crusty from sleep crying. It's tiring, but grief opens up new ways of seeing. It reveals new ways of loving. Time is a slow medicine. There's still hard work ahead.

My doctor's office sits in a multipurpose building on the north end of Lake Harriet. I stop at Mesa Pizza before my noon appointment. I hope the nurse doesn't smell pepperoni on my breath. Instead, she asks if I have a snoring problem.

"Do you wake up often with a rapid heartbeat?"

"Yes. I have my worst anxiety at night, while sleeping."

"Let's take your blood pressure." She motions to my left arm. "Roll up your sleeve, please."

The nurse tightens the Velcro arm band. Her fingers touch in a mothering way. The monitor breathes and pumps and swells. All I feel is where she brushed me. I'm swaddled in warm thoughts of my own mother's disappeared touch. Then, a shiver. Mom? The white machine hisses and beeps me from the trance.

"Blood pressure is good," says the nurse.

I wonder about her. Does she have children of her own? Grandchildren? Does her mother show through in psychic waves like mine? A nurse is a mother. A doctor is a mother. A pilot, a good cop, birds on wires. All trees. The past and future are mothers. The first three letters of moment are mom. This is how I know the present is a mother too.

My doc strolls in. We are the same age. It's a checkup. Ailments spout from my mouth in a baker's dozen. He gives it to me straight, gloves and all. I'm in good physical health. He already knows about my breakdown, and the diagnosis of PTSD. The sleeplessness.

"Sleep apnea is a possibility," he says. "Would you take a sleep study? It's one of those things you have to stay overnight for."

"Certainly."

The doc hands me a sheet of paper. He smiles. I have one hundred other questions that I save for the internet.

Back home I am reading an article about civilization collapsing when my phone battery dies. The opening measures of "Ease on Down the Road" from *The Wiz* soundtrack come on. I take a day bath. Amid the bubbles I have fun inventing instant classics such as "Ease on Down the Soap."

After the tub, I put on a sport coat for no reason. No reason is the best reason to get dressed up. Preparedness creates.

I get a text from one of the top horn players in town, Ingrid.

"Want to get Taco Riendo?"

"Yes!" I knew I dressed up for a reason.

El Taco Riendo means The Laughing Taco. There is a running taco on the sign over the door. It is super crowded inside. Nobody is running or laughing. There's nothing funny about waiting in a long line.

"I'm just going to get three orders of fries," I say. I could have said anything. She isn't listening.

"Sounds great."

The menu has her full attention. "Ooh, chocoflan. I bet that's good. Hi, my name is Ingrid. I'm going to eat all the things."

"Is food more important than music?"

"I have a system. Top shelf is music, food, and sex. All together in a row, like expensive tequilas."

Huge portions of warm tortillas and fixin's are set on trays before us. All the booths are full, so we take a table in the middle of the restaurant.

The walls appear to be decorated by an interior design student with thirty-five bucks at a rummage sale. Ingrid motions at some objects arranged on a table, including a porcelain Jesus. "Isn't it interesting how Jesus is standing next to a giant mug of Corona?"

"He parties, obviously. Did you gig yesterday?"

"Yeah. It was fun. People danced."

She gathers together her existence from various sources: her own gigs, jobbing on other people's gigs, and teaching. For a while, she played brass section in an orchestra, but it didn't vibe. We're all feeling our way in the dark.

It is nice to spend dinner in such company. The food is delicious. Tejano music plays. There's a TV on a steel arm in the corner. It gives the restaurant that hospital room flair. On the screen a man is holding a computer like a baby.

"You think dancing makes people happy, or happy people dance?" I wonder.

"Yesterday, I was at the post office, and a Michael Jackson song came on. I didn't even realize I was dancing." Ingrid shakes her shoulders side to side. "When I got to the counter, the woman behind me said, 'Girl, nobody can stay still when Michael Jackson's on.'"

"I like 'Ease on Down the Road' from *The Wiz*. Michael sings that one. It makes me happy."

"Want to be happy? Listen to anything by Mozart."

"Anything? *Requiem*?" I pull the last bits of cheese from my plate.

"Yes. Vivaldi is also fun. Again, even though he wrote all these songs for young girls in the conservatory, much of his music is in the minor key."

We hit each other up whenever the classical station is playing a great Sibelius tone poem or Aaron Copland. Then we discuss the local music scene, which is spirited and dynamic and ours. There's no need to complain about those around us who are only in it for the booze, sex, or social status. We both know that if you're not in it for the music, this business will devour you.

"I'll be right back."

I hop to the front counter and order chocoflan. It is different than the picture on the wall. There is a thick layer of flan on the bottom, yellow cake in the middle, and fudge on top.

"Flan is the only crème brûlée I can afford," I say.

"Crème brûlée is overpriced in America. Not in Paris," she says. "And there, it's much bigger."

The dessert is big enough to split ten ways. Each bite sends sugar rushes all the way to the toes.

"All America could come up with is pudding and moist cake mix."

"That is one of the grossest-sounding words," she says.

"Pudding?"

"Moist."

To think if I never put a sport coat on, I'd have said no to tacos when Ingrid texted. I put a necklace on, too. The silver spikes weigh light against my chest and jangle together when I laugh. Autumn is full throttle. The day is getting dark earlier. In the span of our dinner, the city has become a shadow.

On the way out, I high-five the porcelain Jesus. Ingrid and I hunch in our thin coats and shiver. Gusts of wind blast through the holes in my ripped jeans. In the distance, sirens. I'm triggered. A flashback haze takes over. I see Dad opening the door to the police. He says nothing. He knows what they've come to say. Then I'm at the scene of it. An ambulance is being loaded. It's Mom. A rush surrounds me. Nausea. I blink across time-space back to Central Avenue. Ingrid is saying something, but that siren washed it out. The siren has faded.

In the van, we listen to Sly and the Family Stone's "Dance

to the Music." The funk brings my heart back to the moment. Back to the city. Back to Minneapolis.

"Love that beat and those horns!" Her head bobs to the rhythm. "This groove cuts all the way through. In popular music, especially hit songs, simplicity is where it's at."

We get on the freeway. Sly continues to the vocal breakdown. The whirl of my van tires are in key with the a cappella voices.

"This the most famous part of the song, the non-lyrics," she says. "Do doo—do doo—do do doo."

"Nonsensically sublime, as Howard Devoto put it."

"Also, I love hand percussion." Ingrid does a bucket seat dance as we barrel down the interstate. It is a deleted scene from *Footloose*.

The asphalt beneath us is fresh with sleet. It sprays the surrounding cars as we speed by them. My window doesn't close tight. A whistle sings in my left ear. Everywhere is music. Somewhere under the Indian Ocean is a white whale that knows nothing about our mixed-up musical methods. Yet it sings. Somewhere in deepest Africa an elephant knows nothing about topping the charts. Yet it sings.

I'm back home when a timer chimes. My shoes that squeak on linoleum are musical too. The furnace blows. The house breathes. I sleep.

Thursday morning, Maurice asks for a ride to the music shop to return a broken tape recorder. He doesn't have a driver's license. When I pick him up, he is wearing a fullbody cat onesie.

"Can I smoke in the van?" he asks.

"Depends on how flammable that cat costume is."

"Got this for Halloween. Now I wear it all the time." He rolls the window open.

"Maurice, you smell like my grandpa."

"Your grandpa smelled like weed?"

"No. Cigarettes and Wisconsin."

He reminds me of Milwaukee in a time I'd never been. Maurice could have been Dad's childhood friend who sneaked in the back door of movie houses with him. Then again, I don't think Dad ever had a friend with a full-body cat suit. But we all have secrets.

"I'm telling you, man, I'm never taking this thing off." It's impossible to stop Maurice from being Maurice. If you try to, you'll miss his beauty.

"Gray is a good color on you."

"Yep."

He sucks on a cigarette and flicks it onto the road. "Don't get white, because white gets dirty."

"Or you could just wash it."

I hit the gas and the speakers at the same time. St. Vincent is singing "Digital Witness." We turn left on Lyndale. It's a short trip. He could have walked, but I enjoy the company.

Maurice goes into the music shop. I wait outside. Lucky for me, JM comes strolling down the sidewalk. JM is my main guitarist. When he plays a solo, clouds part. Smoke machines break. There is a metaphysical field around him. I leave my coat off to feel the last of the warm wind. Something soapy is in the breeze. A cleanness. Musicians tend to notice this foreign aroma called soap. JM's silken hair lilts with the finesse of a freshly washed guitarist.

"I played a dinner gig last night," he said.

"How'd that pay?"

"It's good. This month I'm making adult money."

"That's great."

"You should pick that gig up, man."

"I dig jazz, but right now I'm only doing happy music."

"What do you mean? Jazz is happy."

Kids with guitar cases rotate in and out of the store. They all wear the same blue flannel from generations ago. The one we wore when grunge was the thing. Maurice emerges. JM's mystery soap smell is overtaken by a weed smell.

"They got to process my return? They sold me a broken recorder, what's to process? I don't get it, man."

"Damn. That's a drag, buddy."

JM steps around the corner and into the store. "See you at rehearsal, Mall-Man," he shouts.

"Who was that?" Maurice asks.

"It's my guitarist, JM. You probably don't recognize him in street clothes."

"Dude smells good. Clean."

"I know, right?"

Next, we slag around the art museum to kill time. Upstairs, we see violent paintings of religious atrocities. Maurice talks at great length of Anabaptist hysteria in sixteenth-century Germany. The full-body cat onesie is a detriment to his credibility.

"I bet every painter in this museum smoked weed," he says.

With great restraint, I do not touch the beckoning landscape of *Olive Trees with Yellow Sky and Sun* by Vincent van Gogh. I've exercised this restraint since art school. The painting still grabs at my hand with a secret tractor beam. I pull away before the alarm sounds. Dearest Vincent, you are my Superman. The popularity of impressionism was just on the horizon when you left. If you could see us now, gushing over this work, maybe you'd have kept fighting.

"Once I thought Van Gogh sold only two paintings," I say. "The more I research, the less certain the number. Guess how many works were commissioned, sold, or traded for other paintings?"

"How many?"

"Nobody knows. Which painting was his last?"

"Which one?"

"Nobody knows. Did he actually shoot himself in the stomach?"

"Nobody knows?"

A myth of suffering enshrouds the great painters. It's preposterous to assume all great art is conceived in torrid, emotional squalor. It's clear from the work that Van Gogh painted with his heart. His painting is bright, sunny, and dripping wet. It's as if he sneaked out of the room just beforehand. Someday I will catch him and say thank you for inspiring the world.

I would like to treat Van Gogh to some Dairy Queen. Our strawberry cheesecake will resemble the sky in *Olive Trees*. We will ooze into one another like human paint. The sky will become a spaghetti twist of ruby and tangerine. Surrounding us will be a frame painted in gold. Below the painting, a card will read *The Ice Cream Eaters. Oil on Canvas. Date Unknown.*

Maurice and I walk down a marble hallway and marvel at a hyper-realist painting of Muhammad Ali.

"A museum is a mausoleum," I say.

"Look at all these fancy paintings. When musicians die, we're basically forgotten."

"Not Prince."

"Exception."

The most purply painting at this place is *View of Dresden: Schlossplatz* by Ernst Ludwig Kirchner. I have no idea what Schlossplatz means, but my guess is grape soda. It is a little-known fact that Kirchner augmented his paintings with grape soda, where his other contemporaries used linseed oil. If you doubt me, go smell one. When the guard asks what you're doing, say, "I'm smelling the Schlossplatz."

"Hey, man, I love the museum, but today is my only day off. I want to get high at some point," Maurice says.

"Absolutely. Let's cut out. This crap ain't going anyplace. It's closing in five minutes anyway."

We take the stairs past the museum restaurant. I was fired as a cashier there in college. Never be good at something you wouldn't want a career in.

In the parking lot, I put on "Happy" by Pharrell.

"What do you think of this song?" I ask.

He bursts out laughing. The ears on his cat costume flop around. "Musically or sarcastically?"

"I think it's well written," I say. "It's got a solid groove too."

"Structurally, sonically, and emotionally, it's perfect. Pharrell figures out these perfect pop formulas."

"Do you like it?"

"I can't relate, man. When I was growing up, tragedies were what made me play music. I related to musicians or songs that expressed anger, sadness, and confusion."

"So it doesn't make you happy?"

"This song is a joke. There's no dirt. No grit. It's not human. Plus, I'm not happy. But who is?"

"It makes me feel good."

"Good for you then."

After dropping him off, I call the costume shop about animal onesies. They are out. When I get home, the duplex is grey inside. Autumn rain taps on the windows. My piano is set up in the corner. I play fast songs slow, waiting on the microwave. The tail on the Kit Cat clock moves in sync with its eyeballs. Left. Right. Left. Right. Hypnosis.

The next day is sunny cold. It's a superb morning to be an indoor plant. Plants know secrets to happiness. They keep reaching toward the light. There's a message in there. If you find yourself in some corner, bend so the greatest amount pours on you. Don't punish yourself for wanting to give up. Wanting to give up and giving up aren't the same.

Be serene. Stretch. Stay hydrated.

I drive to the coffee shop to meet my buddy Jones. I wonder what his take is on Pharrell's "Happy." Jones isn't active in any hip scenes anymore, but he still performs the hours away like the rest of us. With tough golden skin and hair black as a record, the guy has played in the same band for forty-two years. In Minneapolis before the Minneapolis sound, there was a piano in every lobby of every hotel in town. Jones says it was great for sniffing up cash.

Through the window the trees are on fire with autumnal blaze. The scene in the trees is fire while they ready for sleep. A leafy, midafternoon sunset. I buy a steamer in a to-go cup with almond milk and sugar-free caramel syrup. It fogs my glasses. That's why they call it a steamer. The heat shocks my system awake. Our table is unstable. I step on the leg so our drinks won't spill.

"What do you think of the Pharrell song 'Happy'?"

"When I first heard that song, it did make me happy. I remember watching him get choked up on TV, talking about how it affected people. It's powerful."

"Powerfully annoying?"

"A long time ago there was a song 'Don't Worry Be Happy,' which annoyed people because it was played too much. They say, 'Don't sweat the small stuff, and everything is small stuff,' but if you heard a song quote that ten times a day . . ." He raises his eyebrows.

"Songs don't have to hit you over the head to be effective. That's if you, me, Pharrell, Lana Del Rey, or whoever intend to write a song of such effectiveness to begin with."

"A lyric about lying on the beach might be enough to get your mind off walking through two feet of snow," Jones says.

He speaks in guided meditations. Always about some beach somewhere. The lines on his face are etched by slugging it out in piano bars year after year. It wouldn't be hard to write sheet music on him. "Who's Lana Del Rey?" he adds.

The drink heats my belly and my belly heats my skin. Relaxation comes in percentages. When it drifts, I drift with it. I find new ways to invite it in. Meeting with Jones is one such activity.

"Do you feel music has shaped your mind over time?" I ask.

"In big ways. Everything from the low animal brain of your cerebellum bopping along with the rhythm to the higher parts of your brain envisioning a beach somewhere is shaped by songs."

"There's a song by Nine Inch Nails called 'Heresy.' Reznor sings God is dead, nobody cares, and he'll see you in hell. I used to blast 'Heresy' and scream along. It helped. How do you think that shaped my mind?"

"Because it addresses emotions," Jones says. "It's good to get those out. Anger is a natural part of the human condition. We need it to survive."

"Jones, anger makes me angry. I don't like it."

"Grim feelings do exist, and we have to find a way to deal with them. There needs to be a balance of positivity for not what we are trying to avoid but where we are trying to get."

"I'm working to stay happy. I made a Happiness Playlist."

"That's one way. Keep working, but remember balance."

My drink is sweet and creamy and the leaves are floating off the trees outside and the coffee shop is warm and dry and Jones is kind, even if we disagree about grim feelings. We talk about Elvis and surfing till it's time to go. We fist-bump goodbye.

After the coffee shop, I make a tally of happy activities.

I'm going to take a cue from Jones and practice growing the calm to balance my worry. I'll discover how to be on both sides of fear, and visualize switching from one to the other. I'll surround myself with people who lift me up. When I start thinking scary things, I'll steer the mind. I'll tape slide whistles over my vents. I'll take off my socks. I'll watch trees.

Annie and I go to the mall that night. We pass the insurance office where her cube is. We pass the airport. A monstrous Boeing 717 flies dozens of feet over the van. I duck my head for dramatic effect.

"I wonder if anyone has ever tried to stuff a bag of seasoned hot wings onto a plane because they hate airplane food?" I ask.

"Up the butt?"

"I didn't think that far ahead, but yes. Security might pull them aside thinking they caught a drug mule."

"Until they pull out a baggie full of squished hot wings."

"I'd bet the person gets arrested anyways because TSA added flaming hot wings to the suspected terrorist hijack weapons list. Not that I would try it, because I love this country."

"And why waste a hot wing?"

That weekend, six blocks of downtown is quarantined for a horror and music festival. The Zombie Pub Crawl is an annual mega concert where people dress up like *The Walking Dead* and get blasted on party liquor. In the coming hours, 30,000 face-painted slugs will get blitzed off their undead butts. It's a corpse's Cabo Wabo. Zombies throwing up on storefronts. Zombies making out in pizza lines. Zombie nurses slamming Jell-O shots. Zombie Pokemons with Zombie Richard Nixons passed out in taxis.

Load-in is 5 p.m. Because of the quarantine zone, we drive the wrong way up a one-way to the club.

My band van is called Night Ghost because it's near black. Before Night Ghost were The Silver Bullet and The Steely Van. If I could drive a piano, we'd tour in that.

We load our gear through the side door. The light guy is a longtime peer named Mud. I haven't seen him much, as he is a full-timer in the lighting world and tours a lot. At this point in the business, he goes by Duke. This is a friendly surprise. Mud has shaved his head. He looks like Ed Harris, or in the right light, a death angel. I know him from the time in his life when he got stabbed in the knee.

"Want to eat dinner with us, you bastard?"

"I wouldn't be caught dead with you." Which means yes.

We walk a mile and a half to Grumpy's on Washington Avenue. *Die Hard* plays on the TV on the wall. It makes me sentimental for the holidays. With Dad in Wisconsin, and my brother in LA, my band is my Minneapolis family.

Dinner arrives. The tater tots are steaming from the fryer. Whiskey spills into low-ball glasses. A tall club soda with lime comes for me. Anyone in Minneapolis eating alone is welcome to join us but nobody does.

"You guys doing the Zombie thing tonight?" asks the server.

"Yup."

On TV, Bruce Willis crashes through a glass skyscraper.

"Bloody feet. The worst."

Annie meets up with me at the quarantine zone. It's a mess with costumed drunks. They moan and lope about. The word "Braaaaaaaaains!" echoes from behind a Porta-Potty. We catch a few minutes of Smash Mouth performing "I Can't Get Enough of You, Baby."

Thirty thousand decaying drunks at the Zombie Pub Crawl party hard. Showtime approaches. I'm backstage adjusting my red jeans in the mirror. I slop two gobs of INVISI

Gel Max Hold in my hair and slick it back. The green room window is cracked open. Fake death moans echo up the street.

There is a knock at the door. The stage manager yells, "Showtime!"

The band is on fire. We are in a perfect state of flow. I salute the crowd and picture Bruce Willis hanging off the skyscraper. He sees all of Los Angeles lit up for the holiday. He feels the breeze blow against him in contrast with the fire blazing above. It's perilous and awesome at the same time.

Stretch it over seventy-five minutes, and that's what it feels like to perform a rock show. Then it's over.

I walk off stage and straight out the stage door to the alley to lie on the ground. There are stars up there someplace. My ears scream from tinnitus. Streets rumble. The smell of auto exhaust fills my nose. It feels safe on the concrete. Music has given me confidence that the earth won't crack open and swallow me whole.

Annie texts. She gives me confidence too.

"Great job! I'm going to bike home. Have fun."

It takes three hours to unload the gear and drop off the band. I get into bed at 2:30 a.m. My ears ring. Music vibrates up to the nerve endings of my teeth. Face in pillow, I dream that the world's last surviving newspaper headline reads "Local Cryogenist Keeps Rock Music in a Jar for Future Wedding Reception."

During the week, Dad and I talk twice a day, as usual.

"When times are tight, make soup," he says. "One crock of soup can feed a person all week. I'll send you a crockpot, son. You can make chili and soup just like your old man."

"If I leave it on, will it start a fire?"

"No way. You can leave a crock on all week. The worst thing that can happen is your soup dries up."

A day later it comes in the mail. The pot is first-class in size and not cheap. I'll make Dad proud by conjuring historic soups in this cauldron. It will be a nice occupation to soothe winter's grip. Snow isn't far off, even in October. Now is a smart time to hit up the grocery for a season's worth of soup ingredients.

I text Annie.

"Can I put rice in it?"

"Yeah. Carrots too."

"Noodles?"

"Yeah. Noodles are OK. Sour Patch Kids are definitely OK."

"Can I put donuts in it?"

"Yes, you can make donut soup."

"This is my calling."

The soup preps come to sixty dollars in total. That includes some bowls. If I could get by a month on these ingredients, I wouldn't be forced to eat the neighbors. Winter scenarios paint my brain. Soup with the band. Soup dates. Soup with pets. Soup baths.

I text Dad. "What a crock!"

"Glad you're having fun, kid."

When everything is chopped and dumped in the slow cooker, I get nervous. What have I created? How bad will it be? Mom is somewhere laughing. Her baby boy is making his first soup at forty-three years old.

"This is delicious," she'd say, no matter how bad it was.

After she passed, Dad cooked alone for months. He crocked up loads of chili and froze it away, looking out the kitchen window at a still picture. One of my last memories of Mom is seeing her framed by that window from the yard. I have memories from both sides of that window. From outside, as a kid playing in the snow. And from the inside, as a man coming home from Minneapolis through the garage. Mom liked to look out and see the birds while she did housework. An angle of road where the school bus stopped could be seen as well.

"My little baby's home! Are you cold, dear? Dad made soup." She'd smile. "Look, there's a cardinal in the tree."

But what was behind her faraway gaze? Father Kurt said it was between her and God. He said we'd never know the answer. A person wastes time asking why. You can't solve problems with problems. Wise priest.

The sacred crock simmers. Something delicious is brewing in that magic jar. How would my first soup taste?

I call Dad.

"It'll be good, relax," he says. "You can't screw up with a crock. We had a big slow cooker at work. In the morning we'd dump some corned beef, cabbage, potatoes, and chopped onion in the sucker. By eleven we'd all be sitting around a table eating delicious lunch."

"I bet that was the tastiest."

"Your mother had a crockpot she liked for a long time."

"I remember. It was round and white, with vegetables painted on the side."

Dad's voice perks up when we talk about her. "Yes! It had a brown knob and a brown cover. She'd call me at work and say, 'Don't forget to turn the crock off when you come home.' Sometimes I'd forget, though."

"But it still tasted good?"

"When your mother cooked, it always tasted good. Because it was your mother."

It's true. Mom made crêpes with blueberries on Saturdays. She made chocolate chip cookies with walnuts and deep-dish pizza in a cake pan. Mom sang when I played piano while she cooked stuffed green peppers or pumpkin pies. She was strong and emotional and liked to go dancing. When I was five, we sang "Rockin' Robin" in the car. She taught me how songs heal. In her final months, she cried to me. Buried deep in her sorrow, the music was still there. Maybe it's what she became after she died.

The crockpot makes the kitchen smell like a genuine home. Every half hour I come up from the studio, worried about a soup fire. By sunset it is time. I fill a bowl up. The onions and carrots are soft and tasty. It is a fair success. I take pictures.

One crock of food gets me through three days. What frugal genius invented this magical machine?

Obviously, witches. Cauldrons are all the proof I need.

My phone rings. It's Annie.

"Hi, Mark. I wanted to . . ." She pauses. "I wanted to call and tell you in advance, I made plans tonight. I'm going to Icehouse tonight for a show. So you might not want to go there."

"On a date?"

Again, silence. Light years of the stuff. I slump against the cupboard in the wall. My head withers along the warped wood. I say nothing.

"It's hard for me, too, Mark. But I figured you should know, so I didn't surprise you if you ended up there."

"I'm sorry for whatever I did to contribute to this. I love you so much."

"You didn't do anything at all. No apologies."

"How did it ever get to this place?"

"We agreed on this, remember? Have a good night."

"Good night, Annie."

She's right, I can't beat myself up. There's never a right time to talk down to yourself. I'm debating a tattoo that says "Crying for No Reason Is OK."

Wonderful Annie, honest and true, even after a breakup. A layer of electricity forms between my muscles and skin. Anxiety. My nose stings from fighting tears. Worry and fear are created in the mind. The brain is constant in having to create the mind. It babysits itself. There's no standard to anxiety, which is why there's no standard to fixing it. Squirrels know this. They risk their lives on electrical wires because they understand balance.

I go for a walk along Minnehaha Creek. Vibrant impressionist water diffuses a scene of urban woodlands. If Monet were alive today, there would be Doritos bags and crushed beer cans in his paintings too. In the water, I see one small lost fish.

"Pay attention, and look at all that appears. That's the way it works if you watch for the details," Dad says.

So that's what I do. The longer I look into the creek, the more fish I notice, the more beauty I discover. I feel better. I also discover there are soup stains all over my pants.

When I get home, the playlist is going. It's Whitney Houston's "I Wanna Dance With Somebody." I have nobody to dance with, so I have a bunch of soup alone. That's nice, too, in a different way.

On Friday I have rehearsal. Sonic booms shake loose any rust around our bones from the week. JM's wiry hands graze the guitar as if through hot dish water. It is too graceful. Grace is a thing that doesn't belong in my rock show. I stop the song.

"Why the hesitation?" I ask.

"I'm worried about going over the top."

"There is no such thing."

"I don't want to step on your toes, though."

Darren, the drummer, points at me with his stick. "He steps on his keyboard all the time."

"Step, man. Stomp."

We run through the song again. This time he shreds. Rehearsal finally sounds as it should, like a construction site.

Friday night flickers on. It's Halloween weekend. Ingrid calls. She's going to a release party for a book. It's a concert party at First Avenue, on the 7th St. stage. I join her. We are two R-rated movie buddies on the loose. There is nothing romantic between us. I'd never date another musician. It would be like two spiders trapped in a glass jar.

"What's with this rain-not-rain stuff?"

"It's called October."

Street neon reflects in puddles. A drunk limps by, her mouth an open airplane hangar. It is the type of mouth that whistles when breathing. It exists independent of the body.

"The living dead," I say.

"It's just kids having fun, Mark."

"Not sorry. I'm a wet grump. Bah!"

We get to the show. Some sexy trophy boy in a white tee sways side to side on stage. The kid is crazed, knees wobbling and throbbing in time. He used to be me. I lean on the bar, and wait for a water. Got to shake these grumps. Science says hold a smile long enough and it becomes real. My argument is, when a goldfish swims in a tank of grape soda, does the goldfish become grape soda? Even so, I force a smile. It works.

Later, we head to the Depot Tavern. Motorhead blares from stereo speakers over the bar. Lemmy sings about how he doesn't want to live forever. I do. The restaurant is packed. We walk out. The street is bustling despite the rain. Midnight brings an urban smell of concrete forests.

"Want to go to a costume party?" I ask.

"Sure."

We speed across town. The heat rushes louder than the radio. "California Stars" by Billy Bragg and Wilco plays. The freeway is wet and shiny. In a month it will be iced.

We haven't any costumes, but it doesn't matter. All parties are the same. We bring a box of cookies from the gas station. BYOC. After a hundred wondrous snapshots of nothing happening, we leave.

Early a.m. traffic rolls along. Ingrid and I are both too tired to talk. The last thing we agree on before I drop her off is that at least it isn't snowing.

At night I dream that deep soot clouds cover up the city. "All they manufacture are ashes," says Ingrid. I throw a snowball at nothing in the parking lot and miss.

Two nights later it's Halloween. The earth is gray with sleeping trees. I see a runaway dog. It appears to be laughing. Frightened dogs get mistaken for happy ones. Beyond that, is laughter even happiness? The wicked witch doesn't laugh because she's happy. She's happy because she is evil. Music isn't like that. It's not misleading. Music can only be music.

Annie is in Brooklyn visiting a friend. We've made a plan not to text each other. It's difficult, but I must learn to be single again. The plan is to try to have fun all by myself. I slip on my white jumpsuit. It's airbrushed with a spoon and cherry on the back. Emoji sunglasses finish off the costume. I'll tell people I'm Meta Elvis. Nobody asks.

There are seven parties to attend. There is a party overlooking the freeway from a hill, and one around a fire where rappers gather. My favorite party serves undercooked brownies. I cram some in the jumpsuit pockets and forget about them.

Maurice is standing in the front yard.

"Mallman, I'm hiding. Shhh!"

"Dude. I can see you."

He wears dreadlocks, a red union suit, and googly eyes taped to his hair. "I'm a Rock Lobster."

"You look like Howard Stern in red pajamas. What happened to your cat onesie?"

"I washed it and it fell apart."

He staggers inside. I get in my van.

Uptown McDonald's isn't on the way home, but I'm craving a number two. To clarify, that's two cheeseburgers, fries, and a medium-sized lithium battery acid.

"$5.22. Please pay at the second window."

While waiting, I watch a neon party bus bounce down Hennepin Avenue. Grown adults dangle out the window. They shout wolf cries and drool Rumple Minze onto the street below.

At the window, the employee pauses. "That looks fun."

"When you're older, you'll be glad you worked instead of partied."

The car behind me honks. I drive away.

At the stoplight, a fake Rastafarian sways. When the light turns green, it matches the color of his nausea. His mouth swings open, eyes wide to the sky.

Back on Cedar Avenue, a suspicious minivan is stopped in the road. A batch of greasy-eyed teenage freaks cackle inside as I pass. Then smack, an egg hits my side window.

A volcano of white hot fire blasts through me. I smash the horn, crush the gas pedal, and give chase. The side streets are wet and slick. I am a caveman on wheels, entangled in a savage, swerving, downright wicked van chase. With teenagers. Fumbling one-handed, I attempt to get a photo of their license plate but the automatic flash is on. All I can get out of my mouth is "You!"

Our vans whip through residential streets. I have one hand on the horn, and the other on my phone, chasing them down an alley, driving with my knees again. Meanwhile, my camera is taking flash photos of the dashboard.

I let go of the picture idea. What now? Ram them into a light post? Sideswipe them off the river bridge? By this time they are gaining distance. I decide to throw something. In back is my thirteen-pound bowling ball. I can't risk its bouncing off a side panel and back into me. Plus, I'd paid extra to have my name engraved on it. Instead, I chuck a half-full bottle of ibuprofen. It bounces off the road and opens; 200 mg tablets spray over my windshield.

We jet out the alley and back onto Cedar. My final recourse, and last resort, are the cheeseburgers. The first one falls out of its wrapping mid-launch. Part of the bun clings to my hood. The kids are far away by this point but I throw the second burger on principle. It bounces sadly. I run it over. A pair of taillights rounds the corner blocks away. They are out of sight. It is no use throwing the fries.

I pull over to the side of the road. My hands shake. I morph back into my adult self. What have I become? Giving chase and letting go was the best-case scenario. Even if I did catch them, what then? Beat up teenagers? More likely I'd have gotten beaten up by them. The mind doesn't fully develop the ability to assess risk until age twenty-five. What is my excuse? That's when I realize it was them who let me go.

On the couch watching *Labyrinth* is how Halloween ends. I breathe deep, close my eyes, and eat a fry.

November

The goal of each day is to worry less. Songs come in dreams. I rush to my studio and hit record before they fade. Nobody will hear them. They are as private as the dreams that birthed them. If you can't keep your own secrets, how do you know you can trust yourself?

After I capture the dream songs, breakfast comes with the heat cranked and windows open. Delicious oatmeal and blueberries. Worry flies off to bother some other guy.

Annie invites me to the airport dog park in the afternoon. This is good timing. I'd hoped to talk more about us. Would she be open?

The day is warm and it is nice to joke with her again. One would think jet roars would make the place unpopular, but dogs just want to party.

"All dogs are naked," she says. "Look at all these nude heathens running around."

"If I came to the dog park naked, I'd get kicked out."

"You'd totally get arrested."

We walk on a carpet of dead leaves as her terrier mutt eats mud.

"Gilligan, don't eat that!" He ignores her. "I should open a dog restaurant."

"You might want to be more specific with the wording."

"A restaurant *for* dogs," she waves her arms. "Gilligan, gross!" He peeks up with muddy lips and trots beside us. "People won't be welcome. The doors would be made small so only dogs can fit."

"What type of music would play in there?"

"Kendrick Lamar. Dogs like all the same stuff I do."

"'Who Let the Dogs Out?'"

"I don't like that song," she says. "Neither do dogs. It's not even really about them."

The three of us walk to a marsh that separates the airport from the freeway. Dusk begins. The sun is going down earlier every day. It wasn't the perfect time to bring us up. But when would be?

"Annie," I take the chance. "I'm sorry it all went in the crapper."

"Ohhh, it's not your fault." She touches my back. "You've brought so much joy into my world."

"I don't want to let go or move forward. I want to pick one day in history and repeat it."

"Change is . . ." Airline howls grumble in the sky.

"What?!"

The sky goes quiet again. A summer breeze blows across the airstrip and onto our shoulders. The sky goes quiet again. It is 77 degrees in November. Meteorologists across the metro are having nervous breakdowns.

Her voice softens. "Change is part of life, Mark." Annie's voice is quiet and kind. "It makes me nervous, too, but we will always be solid. We'll keep doing fun things."

Goosebumps spread across my bare arms. "There's nobody like you." I'm holding back tears. The doggo whips in half circles around us.

"I care about us." She stops and looks into my eyes. "I

wish it were different. You're not alone. I get emotional about us, too."

We hug by the exit gate. Gilligan's leash tugs at Annie, pulling her away. He doesn't want to leave the park. I don't want to leave the relationship. Annie's heart beats against mine. Behind her, I see a gold world. Our hug is so long it would be edited for television.

On the drive home, we pass a three-car accident on the bridge. Nobody is hurt. Traffic slows to get a snapshot of the damage. A man in a KISS T-shirt is offering hunks of a candy bar to the others as we drive by. They all turn him down.

"Did you see that? The one guy was offering pieces of a candy bar to the victims. They were all refusing," I say.

"I wouldn't take candy from some dude who hit my car either."

She drops me off. Gilligan tries to jump out with me. Inside, I put on "Ooh Child" by the Five Stairsteps. It's a song Mom sang. If I came home with a broken something, she'd hug me and sing, "Ooh, child, things are gonna get easier." The song moves up my shoulders and brings a chill as my bones open. I take four deep breaths. My phone vibrates. It's a message from Ingrid. A link to a *New York Times* article reads "Dalai Lama: Behind Our Anxiety, The Fear of Being Unneeded." How did Mom get ahold of Ingrid's phone to message this? I read the whole thing twice, once for Ingrid, and once for Mom.

I hum to myself. "Ooh, child, things are gonna get easier."

Over the week, songs are conceived, and others buried. Soup smells waft about.

On Wednesday, I play a laughable game of one-on-one with Maurice at the Y. In the parking lot, I get a message from Eugene inviting me over for a poodle walk. I love our walks because he is a gracious listener.

Eugene is a music writer and podcaster. He has the face of an American black bear, if a bear wore glasses. He stands six foot three. Six foot three and a half in sandals. Eugene's fuzzy hair spirals up, as if he has a beard on his head. This hair tower adds four more inches to his stature.

Eugene occupies a duplex. It's a northeast top and bottom, unlike my south side by side. He shares the bottom half with his fiancée, Jess, and their standard black poodle, Zooey.

He travels the world. I once bumped into him and Jess at the co-op downtown. Eugene wore a long silk robe called a djellaba. He'd bought the djellaba in Casablanca from a rug merchant. We shared a belief that the twenty-first century fashion was a suggestion, not a construct. He was also wearing a Minnesota Twins cap, like the one hanging from the hook in my bedroom.

Initially, we became friends by proximity, when I lived downtown. His loft was opposite the off ramp from mine. There was a parking lot, a wine bar, and a rare-books store between us. Eugene complained about the stodgy book dealer but he'd always go back. Your dealer is your dealer. I didn't make it past the wine bar's flourless chocolate cake to ever get to that book joint.

But big money invaded and pushed us both out of the North Loop. I moved south of the city, and he went northeast. Now he's an eighteen-minute drive away, according to my phone. This new distance tests the tenacity of our friendship.

"Out front," I text.

"Come in," he replies. "Go through the kitchen door around back."

His place carries a sweet musk of used hardcovers and weed. Eugene has more books than he'll ever read. Same is true with weed. There is an atrocious wood carving of a woman's naked torso on the counter by the sink. He picked it up in Santa Teresa, a neighborhood in Rio de Janeiro. Eugene calls it Bunda art, and claims his fiancée has grown to love it. It's an awful, crude thing. I'm certain Jess has not grown to love it.

Eugene stretches out on the sectional sofa with a novel face-down on his belly. His hairy bare feet hang from the edge. How long had he been sleeping?

"Oh, hey. I was just reading," he smiles, rubbing his eyes.

"I was just at the gym, playing basketball." I plop into the recliner. "Scored only one point."

On a coffee table, clumps of pot are piled in a ceramic bowl. A bowl for bowls. Zooey is sniffing about the room, inspecting the house's inner parameters.

Eugene takes amusement when I play sports. "You scored only *one point*? I should run a clinic for you?"

"Clinic? Is that locker room talk?" I pick up a book about F. Scott Fitzgerald and flip through it.

"No, a clinic for shooting, dribbling, and passing."

"So, yes. But, as you know, there's not much passing in one-on-one. Though I do have this special move where I pass it from myself to myself."

I shoot my hands up toward the ceiling. An invisible basketball soars through the upstairs apartment where a neighbor's dog is also sniffing parameters, and into the sky. It bounds with light-speed grace until it smacks into the earth's atmosphere. With a sonic boing, my imaginary ball bounces toward earth again. It zooms through a flock of geese, separating their southern V, and creating two intersecting perpendicular rows of birds. An X of geese that crash into each other and fall without grace. The ball smashes silently through the roof and back into my agile hands.

"That's a double dribble, Mark."

Eugene sets the hardcover on the coffee table next to the Kush. "I started playing real organized basketball on the seventh-grade traveling team." He slides his feet into a pair of brown grandpa sandals.

"A traveling team? That's a foul, Eugene." The poodle trots over to sniff my parameters.

"One day, the coach came off the court and asked me in a hushed voice, 'Do you know what you're doing out there, Eugene? Do you?' And obviously not. I stared at him. My whole high school basketball career I played nervous, always scrambling to catch up instead of forcing the action myself. That guy sucked the game away. Made basketball into a struggle for survival. It wasn't until college, without him crouched on the sidelines, that I played aggressive and well."

I slam the Fitzgerald book shut. "Dammit, coach!"

"He gave the game a false importance." Eugene shakes his head. "I choked. But it wasn't the coach; it was me. I was choking myself."

"Happens in the studio to musicians. It's called red-light fever."

"In sports, it's called flop sweat."

Eugene rattles a dog leash. Zooey prances to his side.

"It takes a while to get past all that," I say. "When I became at peace with red-light fever is when it began to fade away."

We head out the back door, dog first. The mandarin sun drenches us in splendor. The sky is blown out white as my pupils adjust from the dim. In this lovely moment, I'm impervious to sadness. My eyesight returns.

"I read that Prince preferred to record vocals alone, or with one engineer. Even Prince was sensitive about recording vocals. Even Prince," Eugene says.

"Before we go any further, let's not assume any one thing to be totally true about Prince or his royal methods. He was an enigma, and enigmas radiate mythology. If anything, I bet he caused more red-light fever than anything."

"True."

The park is glowing with auburn trees. Yellow and brown leaves spin off branches among dropped company. In springtime when a bud yearns to become a leaf, it does so in moments of slow majesty. The summer months of clinging on through cloudbursts and tempest gales are triumphant. But autumn is when a leaf comes to full fruition in a single moment of letting go. It arcs and zigzags and undulates a great performance on its way down. The grand finale. The last dance. As the tree becomes naked, each leaf gets a few short seconds of dancing. Then it's over. Humans are lucky to dance as often as we choose. A leaf falls once.

"I've had the fever with some pianos," I say.

"From your childhood? Your relationship to your mother, and how she taught you?"

"No. Piano is frustrating because there's eighty-eight keys and only ten fingers. When a guitar chord is strummed, every string is used. Nothing is wasted. But the only way to hit every note on the piano at once is to lie on the thing."

"Control. You want power."

"Power? You keep your dog on a leash, but it doesn't mean you're power hungry, does it?"

"Well, no, but . . ."

". . . but yes, you are right. You know how a piano has hammers inside? I got hammers inside me too. Believe it."

It wasn't as a child I smashed keyboards. But the tension grew as I did. Slamming fists was organized chaos. Primal catharsis. Unplaying. Unlearning.

The dog poops in the park. Conversation is impossible

when a dog craps. The same thing happens when waiting for a shoe tie or a plane passing over. These are the pause buttons of modern living.

Zooey's legs shake and buckle. She glances around with embarrassed wide eyes. Of all the disgusting tasks a dog accomplishes, why is this act so embarrassing? It eats its own puke. A dog will gallop across the yard chomping frozen turds in January, tail wagging the whole way. It has no shame looking you in the eyes while humping a recliner cushion. A dog will even stop eating, lick its own genitals, then resume eating. What baffles the mind is that all this is no big deal. Yet dropping a load in the park gives it red-light fever.

Eugene bags the poop and tosses it in a garbage can. The poodle is grinning. She sniffs around the base of the trash barrel.

"Two points!"

"I have this recurring dream. The Rolling Stones invite me to join the band. Not on piano, but guitar. Mick introduces me for a solo, and every note is the wrong note. The dream ends backstage with Charlie Watts saying, 'Right on, mate! Right on!'"

"A worship anxiety dream. In John Fine's book *Your Band Sucks*, he says great performers want to be worshipped."

"Thank you."

"Take Prince. There was this *Oh my god* thing going on around him. With fans. With critics. Everybody simultaneously worshipping and fearing Prince. It's an attribute of godliness. Now that he's become eternal, even more so."

A kid is shooting hoops alone on a basketball court.

I motion at him. "What about basketball? LeBron James isn't out there killing the game because he wants to be worshipped. He's doing what he loves."

"Yes, but Michael Jordan wanted to humiliate and destroy the opponent. He was a power-hungry dominator."

The kid makes every shot in five minutes. He dribbles a drum beat and shoots a three-pointer. We clap from the bench.

"So, in musician terms, Michael Jordan was a solo artist. LeBron James is in a band."

"Exactly. Jordan is the model for basketball success. A big scary superstar. Great at everything, but a lonely figure."

"Who is happier?"

"LeBron. He loves the idea of community. He's also a great passer."

With that we spend the rest of the afternoon contemplating the wind. What if all the money in the world blew away someday? We didn't choose our careers; they chose us.

The next morning I stay in bed till noon swiping on my phone. I put on The Happiness Playlist. "Can I Kick It?" by A Tribe Called Quest plays. It pumps me up, and I spring from the bed. The music makes me feel strong, like a flower. Strong with the ability to manufacture joy where once was nothing. I open the windows and turn up the thermostat. The outside blows through. Serenity pours down my spine in time with the music. I open a jar of almonds and get lost in the beauty of the waking dream around me.

Out the window I watch a squirrel observing Cedar Avenue. In still sunlight, we both twitch our heads to spy a truck in the alley and slow cars on the move. We both scratch our backs. Yawn. Survey the crystal sky. I don't know how much time passed, but it was half a jar of almonds worth.

Dad calls.

"Hey, buddy."

"Hi, Dad."

"You busy? I want to tell you a funny joke."

"Nah. Just eating almonds and watching a squirrel." I grab a broom and sweep around.

"There are these two guys in hell. They're sitting halfway up to their necks in crap. The one guy says 'Well, this ain't so bad,' then the boss comes over and yells, 'OK, break's over, everybody back on their heads!'"

"Ha. That's classic."

"Did I ever tell you that happened to me once?"

"You stood on your head in crap?"

"My dad and I were digging a foundation for a house where a farm stood at one time. I was walking around and I fell into a hole. It was where the outhouse was. I was covered."

"My god. For how long?"

"I was able to crawl out," he says. "Good thing I didn't die. My dad made me ride in the bed of the truck the whole way home."

"Was he pissed off?"

"Not that time. But when I took all the clocks apart in the house he was."

"Did you get them back together?"

"Yeah, but they didn't work. Ha ha. My whole life I've been fascinated with mechanical things. Have you ever heard of a machine called a Bridgeport?"

"What does it do?" I ask, sweeping the dirt pile back under the fridge where it came from.

"It's a vertical milling machine. It can drill, cut, and machine. It's a machine that can make a machine of itself. It's a thing that most represents our experience as people."

We continue on, pondering similarities between people and machines. We talk about assembly lines. We talk about cars. Then onto what's for lunch, and the chances of snow.

While ninja spinning the broom, I knock the open jar of almonds to the floor.

"Oops! Dad, I got to go. Spilled my almonds all over."

The conversation ends with "I love you." I gather up the nuts when out the window I see the squirrel on the branch again. In unlaced boots, I go behind the house and sprinkle the almonds in the yard. The squirrel watches from the tree, unmoving, as if I couldn't see it. Just a guy pouring nuts on the ground. Nothing to see here. I've discovered a new happiness activity. Feed squirrels.

It's time to get some work in for the day. I go down to the studio, to catch songs in a difficult net. Listen. Feel the tug. Reel it in. If it's too small, throw it back.

There's a scarf maker who sings when she felts. "Beautiful songs are in this scarf," she'll say.

Beautiful songs are strong in that they are vulnerable. When they go out into the air, they coat the room in butterfly-wing dust. Early on, I made a rule that I wouldn't write while depressed. After Mom died I didn't write for a year.

My best songs have come to me when I listen for the eternal. When I conjure the nucleus ear. It's most often Saturday. Before dinner. When the room is all sapphire and dust. I let it come, and then I break before it finishes. It's lovely to bask midair of inspiration. Press pause and get drunk on the slapstick of life's comic matinee. Cherish the freedom to put your pen away. Leave the song. Step onto the patio. Watch stars. Eat the last half of donut you were saving. Most importantly, write fulfilling songs. There is enough unfulfilled desire already here.

In order to write what you know, you must go out and get to know things. Build a mountain of truths over time. This way, the last song you write will be the result of every song you've ever written. Make certain to sing through your mouth from your heart, not with your mouth from nowhere. Let the content reveal the intent, but be responsible with your artistic karma. Make even the angry songs beautiful.

I walk out to the backyard. The almonds are gone. I look to the trees and smile.

I'm in bed at 11:11. While staring at the ceiling, I wonder if there will be nightmares. Some nights I wake up soaked in sweat, my heart pounding on the floor next to me. What does it mean? Tomorrow's sleep study will shed some light on the haunted amphitheater behind my eyelids.

I make a wish to spectral vortices. A spell. A prayer.

"Dear great whoever you are: I pray the criminals stay in their own neighborhoods tonight. I pray for Mom, floating around up there; may it be enjoyable. I pray for Dad's happiness, for the health of my brother and his family, for Annie's safety, and for Gilligan the dog who is afraid of bananas. I pray for the squirrels in the yard, that they always outrun traffic. I pray the giraffes in the zoo find a way to sneak in and out at their leisure. I pray an asteroid belt of laughter and joy crashes into the world tonight. I pray the starving children of the world are granted superpowers to rise up and overthrow regimes of dictators. I pray love continues on its exponential path. I pray that we aren't living in a computer simulation. I pray that if we are living in a computer simulation, the afterlife is included. I pray there are dinosaurs on Mars. Are you still there?"

I have a Mom dream. We are in a grocery store. She is laughing. I am crying.

"I miss you. I want to hold you and to sing together again. Why are you laughing?"

"You can have all those things, dear." She takes my hand. "I'll always be here with you in dreams."

The following evening, I drive to the hospital. The sleep study is the easiest type of studying I've done since kindergarten. The worst part is paying thirteen dollars to park overnight. I remind myself that a hospital is a place for healing. There's a lot of positivity between those walls. A sign on the elevator reads "Press B for sleep center after 8 p.m." It's 7:30. Instead of standing there for a half an hour, I press B. The ground-floor elevator goes down. This is when I learned that B stands for basement. Next, I come to an air lock with a doorbell. A light comes on in a plastic bubble. It flashes in my face.

"Name?"

"Mark Mallman."

There is a clicking sound. Then a second clicking sound. Then a third. After a fourth and fifth clicking sound, I am greeted by a woman in hospital scrubs. She has those pale-brown coffee-colored eyes a person with blue eyes gets from drinking too much coffee. Overnight eyes. They are so tired they lack reflections.

"You're early," she says. "That's OK. Dory isn't here yet, though."

Another nurse in a series of nurses who'd save me from my own mind. Two questions weigh on my head like anvils. Who is Dory? And did I leave the van lights on?

She leads me through a waiting area.

"Want a water or a juice before we go to your room?"

"Juice. Grape."

"I'll have Dory bring you one."

Down a hallway are two identical Orwellian rooms. I am assigned room one.

Room one feels somewhere between a luxury hospital and a taped-off Super 8 after a drug raid. A smell of motel bedding wafts through. Room one boasts a lovely theme of plain brown, and no windows. The centerpiece is a sizable brown Sleep Number adjustable bed with a brown end table beside it. Against the wall, a brown task chair sits at a little brown desk. It is all tied together by matching brown carpet. Over the bed, a shiny half-dome camera peers down from the ceiling. To the right of the bed is a tower of wrapped-up wires and pads. I set my bags on the floor. The nurse watches from the hall.

"All electronics are off at 10 p.m. Dory will come by in a while and give you the rundown."

The door shuts. Silence falls. If I don't learn anything more that night, I learn my sleep number is 80.

Dory doesn't make the grand entrance her reputation suggests. Instead, she speeds in with the simple announcement of her name. Then she goes over the procedure.

There are EEGs for my head and EKGs for my chest. It's routine to Dory. Sleep apnea. Snoring. Waking in panic. The signs are all there.

"Once your apneas begin, then I will come in with a breathing mask."

Dory is confident my situation is this. If she's right, it means I'll be sleeping the next half of my life with a mask on my face. The mind refuses to accept the flaws of the body. In this case I prefer trial and error over trial and success.

Next, Dory brings in samples of the masks. I'm really not feeling this sleep apnea idea anymore. These Borg masks are a twisted solution. I'm guaranteed to stay single if I fail this sleep study. Who will take me now with a face-hugging robot over my face?

"Dory, is it possible that it's just snoring?" Turn back! Warning! Danger!

"Possible? Yes. Likely? No."

She walks out the door, then stops.

"Mark, be grateful if all you have is sleep apnea. I've seen people come in with conditions that nobody should have to endure. I'll be back in a bit."

When she returns, Dory fixes me into a proper cyborg for the polysomnogram.

"First, I'm going to attach these electrode pads to your head using glue."

"Glue?"

"It's a gel. You can wash it off at home tomorrow."

Somewhere in the middle of her European cruise story, I lose count of how many electrodes she sticks on.

"And my mother told me the secret to a happy marriage . . ." She glops more paste on my head. "It's to go on an adventure together every six months." This is when I realize I have a happy marriage to Darren, my drummer.

Wires hang off me on all sides. Now she's taping electrodes to my face. This seems a bit much, Dory. Does she get paid by number of electrodes attached? Is this how she affords her happy adventures every six months?

Dory wraps an elastic belt around my chest. Then another for safety. I could double for a worst-case scenario in a TSA training seminar. Dory says I must sleep as much as I can. If I sleep under four and a half hours, insurance won't cover it. But no pressure.

This is also my first night wearing a nose mic. Doesn't Britney wear one of these in her Vegas act? My flesh has no other occupation than being monitored. My mind has none other than to lose itself in dream fields. She fastens the remaining bits of technology together, and with a finishing touch, I am robotic. Ladies and gentlemen, introducing Mallborg.

"If you have to go to the bathroom, I'll hear you through the nose microphone, and come to unhook you. I'm going to head to my station down the hall," Dory says, flipping off the lights.

There is a place beyond blindness. Here is a room that has seen no wind other than air pressure from a door opening and closing. A room that has only known artificial light. A wallpapered chamber steeped in silence. There is no echo when one speaks, like someone talking to you from inside of your ear.

"Can you hear me, Mark?" Dory's voice transmits from a speaker in the ceiling.

"Yes."

"I'm going to give a series of tasks. Can you look right for me?"

I look right.

"Good. Can you look left for me?"

I look left. I look up, then down. I blink a number of times. She asks me to move my limbs in slight ways. There are other things, things I don't remember for they were of no consequence to me. What I remember is the dark. The dead quiet.

Dory watches through the night-vision camera. At her station, she notates my breaths, body positions, heart rate, and states of dreaming. I shut my lids, with Big Mother sending signals via matrix as the brain harvests. I cross into surreal slumber. Things get weird pretty fast. My tongue becomes an eyelash. My cheek drips. The cloud drive-thru has extended its hours to accommodate a Nosferatu burrito habit. Khonsu, the Egyptian god of the moon sings, "Hit the sack, Jack!" Am I walking on stars or wearing shoes made by them? My pinky twitches. With a jolt, I am awake again. The body beckons.

"Hello?" I whisper into the void.

"Do you have to go to the bathroom?"

"Yes."

She unhooks the snake of cables. I'm free. While peeing, I think of Kafka's *Metamorphosis*, which takes place in a bedroom in a house, not a hospital. But the similarity is

Gregor, our protagonist, who has become imprisoned by a new physical form. Instead of waking up a cyborg, he's a cockroach. It would have been happier and more accurate if Gregor woke up a butterfly. I just hope to wake up without a scuba mask on.

Back in my adjustable bed, Dory plugs me in. She leaves, a total eclipse of the door. I dream for I don't know how long. There is no way to tell in darkness with no clocks. What if I'm asleep for only one minute? What if for less? How do I know I'm even awake? Pitch dark conjures unreality, a hunger in the eye to know we are not dead. I pinch my hand and count pretend stars that glitter.

A new voice calls out. It isn't Dory.

"Mark?"

"Yes?"

"We are finished. I'll come in and get you ready to leave."

Who is this different nurse? What have they done with Dory? Did room two eat her?

The lights flash on. A blinding, fluorescent sunrise. The different nurse marches in. I squeeze my eyelids, waiting for the eyes to adjust. A cave being exposed to fire. Daylight in a world faster than the body. I beg of you, somnologists, support your local dimmer-switch supplier.

"Dory went to the ER about an hour ago." The brash new nurse yanks my pads off. "She didn't feel well."

"Nobody put a mask on me in the night." My face, hands, side, head, and legs, were globbed with gunk. "Was that because I didn't have any sleep apneas?"

"Too few apneas for a mask." She tugs wires from the goop. "But you move your legs in your sleep a lot, Mark. It's like you are running. If you're running in your sleep, that will make you tired."

This was my diagnosis, sleep running? What if the sleep

center was jacked by hoodlums as I dozed? What was this impostor trying to cover? I want my Dory back.

"The doctor will go into more detail at your follow-up next week. Make sure to wash your hair with hot water before you shampoo, the paste is water soluble. I'll see you at the front desk."

I repack my gym bag, put on my pineapple tank top and ripped coat. As I emerge from the brown womb, the hallway breathes. The sleep center is all heat vents and small talk. The daytime nurses are less soft. Not mothering, just working. They gab and suck coffee at a station behind a half wall. One shoves a green form at me. I fill it out, and leave through the air lock. Another glue head out the door.

A thousand nights I've spent away from home. Never with such a lack of light, white noise, or air.

Coming out of the elevator to the parking ramp is a rebirth. I'm surprised to find it has stormed. The magic of soundproofing. This is why they put sleep centers in the basement of hospitals and not on the roof. Overhead, gray-green pillows hang from lightning rods. They reflect in glass puddles on the parking-ramp floor. Silent lightning strikes dash the violet horizon. I dial up The Happiness Playlist, pay thirteen dollars to watch a gate open, and drive away.

On the freeway, I think about my anechoic sleep chamber. The purpose of a room is to be filled. That is how a room is like a heart. I am reminded of a quote by Vincent van Gogh. "There is something inside of me, what can it be?"

It is pleasing to be home. The storm restarts. My bathroom window is open as I wash the EEG paste off my head. Rain pounds on the screen as I scrape the clear gunk from my skin. I wonder how to get inside my head and clean the gunk away. With music? When I turn off the shower, the sound of the rain continues.

Ten minutes later, I'm naked in the living room googling "how to clean the brain." Jets flying over the house blend with the thunder and cars whisking down Cedar Avenue. It's a chaotic sound but also calming. I feel clean.

A week passes. Cold comes. One evening, Eugene and I race through an art opening at a casket factory.

"I prefer sculpture over painting," he says.

"Because it's less cerebral?"

"Very funny." He pats my shoulder with a giant hand. "Because a painting is confined to being a painting. Anything can be a sculpture."

I point at the first random thing I see. "What about that door?"

"Could be."

"What about that crack in the tile, is that a sculpture?"

"Possibly."

"What about that smell, of coffee and linseed oil? Is that a sculpture?"

"That's postmodernism."

We bolt out in record time. The temperature has dropped another five degrees.

"It's cold. A frost will come," I say. "I can taste it."

"It did once already. Last week."

"Winter's loom. Blech. A few days ago it was raining."

"Don't you like winter?"

"I like the sales on shorts."

We get in and drive to dinner. The van warms up fast. The sidewalks of Broadway are less crowded than in previous weeks. Nightlife died as the last leaves fell.

We arrive at LUSH for dinner. It's early enough to snag a dinner table before the DJ starts.

"Busy in here tonight," Eugene says. He waves his monstrous arm to flag somebody. A shirtless waiter approaches.

He is a striking man whose cut frame oozes youth and table settings. Eugene orders a whiskey. I get a club soda with lime.

"God, if I looked as sexy, I'd never wear shirts again, either."

"Mallman, there must be something worthwhile about winter for you."

I'm quiet. I picture romping with my brother in the snow. The drifts went up past my belly. The dog would dive off the porch with a clumpy white beard. Inside, the wind blew sharp against the warm house. I can almost taste the cocoa now. Bedtime was a haven with my family sleeping walls away on either side. In the morning, I'd smile to see more snow drifting down.

"Anything?"

"It all just melted away. Adult winters have been sterile. Methodical. Frigid. Eugene, I don't want my happiest years behind me. What happened to silly happiness? Frivolousness? Random joy?"

"Don't be afraid. Jump back into life." Eugene smiles. "Here comes your food. I bet the waiter has some tips he'd be willing to give you."

After dinner, disco spotlights paint the room in an outrageous prismatic shower. Drinks vibrate on beat to hard techno. Eugene flags a server and orders a fourth whiskey. It is quite a show. Mystery genders shimmy and twist and backflip across the stage. The room is wild and open and pure. A dancer wears nothing but sequined bikini bottoms and brilliant white wings. Another is wrapped in black vinyl under a bathrobe. The cabaret gets gloomy as well. But it's all a celebration. I lose myself in this jungle of bondage and fur. After the show, Eugene has a fifth whiskey. It's like watching a moose try to get drunk. The booze doesn't make a dent.

Too soon we are back out under the far stars. It's colder.

The van turns over slowly. Eugene tells me everything I don't need to know about basketball while it heats up. Then I hit the gas. We tear through the parking lot between two hanging wires.

"Wires!" Eugene shouts. "Jesus, watch out."

I whip around the corner onto bumpy streets.

"Check this out." I play James Brown's "I Got You (I Feel Good)." Here is a funky dude who happens to feel good and knew that he would.

We arrive at Eugene's duplex. He unbuckles and hops out before I come to a complete stop.

"Well, see you," he mumbles and is gone. It's weird.

"Bye, buddy," I yell through a slit in the rolled-down window. Why is he in such a hurry? Is he mad?

The city is hazy through apricot streetlights. Washington Avenue drunks, too hammered to see I'm not a taxi, try hailing me down. They jump out in the middle of the street yelling at me to stop.

"Get out of the road!" I hold the horn. It's the clown apocalypse.

"You Only Live Once" by the Strokes comes on. Major key distortion and drums slashing. I sing along to the first lyric but that's all. "Some people think they're always right."

When the Strokes' seminal first album came out, I was dating the manager of a CD shop, Rachael. It's a dim sum place now. She always tipped me off on new music. When Bowie's *Heathen* was released, we drove all night soaking it in. The turn of the century was fun. A person could make some bank in the business. I'd go in the studio with the band, track a bunch of new songs, have a couple thousand CDs printed, and off they'd go. It's different now.

Rachael and I sat on the roof of my house. We'd talk music till midnight, then go inside and talk about music in bed. "You got to come see the Strokes with me. I think it's a perfect album. Even the title, *Is This It*?" Of course she was right. But I didn't want to go because I wanted to see them. I wanted to go because we were in love. The tiny club was sold out. Julian Casablancas leaned on the mic doe-eyed. Lucid rock. Out-and-out sex. One of the coolest rock shows I've ever seen.

Rachael is a mom now. She has a good office job out in the suburbs. She still wishes me happy birthday.

Fifteen years later, my white duplex waits under starlight. I pull down the alley and into the driveway behind the garage. In the yard, frosted grass means snow soon. When that comes, the house will meld into a membrane of ice. Be careful of your wrists; it stings to scrape. Such are casual dangers. Ankle twists. Faces meet sidewalks. Winter is hardest on the bare skin.

It isn't late. Maybe Annie will text me? She doesn't.

Alone on the edge of the bed, I reflect on how the splendid fall was long. The coming snow would be pillowy and crisp. Eugene is right: it will be nice. When winter arrives, a vortex opens. Flakes skydive out. Seasonal songs round-robin in corner stores and chain gas stations. Joyfulness is in there. I need to jump back into life.

My phone buzzes. Is it Annie? No, it's Eugene. "Hey man, thanks for the fun night. Sorry I ran off so quick. The whiskey caught up with me. Bathroom emergency."

Mystery solved.

Annie doesn't text until the next night. She invites me grocery shopping. Pulling into the parking lot, her car jostles.

"Whoa, there," I say.

"What if your job is to be a speed bump?" she asks.

"Will I have a protective shell? Or be lying unprotected in the road?"

"You climb into a tube, but you'll still feel it."

The last spots are in the back of the lot where cashiers park.

"I'll get my muscles bigger. That way I can push cars off me like Superman."

"You'd get fired, Mark. Your job is to slow cars down. That's all," Annie says.

The store is overcrowded, but that makes it warm. We share a cart. They are out of yogurt. They are out of bread. So much for yogurt sandwiches. Thankfully the grape soda is properly stocked.

"I think I'll be a musician instead of a human speed bump," I say.

"Same difference."

She picks through the cilantro.

"I need peanut butter."

I walk across the store and grab a small tub. Then I come back to Annie with another hypothetical job, a stomper in a cockroach winery.

"Your new job is to make wine out of cockroaches, stomping around in them ten hours a day," I say, squeezing avocados.

"I'm not going to stomp on cockroaches," she says.

"Either you do it or they cut off your feet."

"That's not the job for me. I'm going off the grid."

"It's the post-apocalypse. The grid is gone."

I pile my items onto the checkout conveyor.

"Can you believe they were out of bread? A grocery should be shut down for that. What are people going to eat sandwiches on? Lettuce?"

Every week I ask myself why I shop there, and every week I go back. We load our carts and leave. Annie drops me off. I watch her drive away from the sidewalk, bags of groceries tugging at my shoulder sockets.

Moonlight loosens the bones. The constellation Orion winks above me. A satellite cuts through his midsection. The top half of Orion's body slides sideways and falls out of the sky.

"Snow."

I catch flakes on my tongue the same as my ancestors before hairstyles ruled the earth. At the dawn of holding hands.

In the morning, grass spikes out through iced cotton. All the groundskeepers at all the golf courses in Minnesota are putting their feet up. Traffic moves half time though soupy streets of monochromatic gray. Fully costumed human shapes hunch down crunchy sidewalks. Felt dolls.

It's the day I leave to spend Thanksgiving with Dad in Wisconsin. Cue music. I flip on The Happiness Playlist. Junior Senior's "Move Your Feet" blares.

Daylight shines through the bathroom's frosted glass. I catch myself averting the mirror as I dry off.

My frizzed hair spikes out to the side. I am a cubist painting. "You're gorgeous," I say. "But don't overthink it." I pack a week's worth of dirty socks into a paper bag and put my shirt on inside out.

The drive to Dad's is a slow six hours. Wisconsin scrolls by. I'm leaving home and headed home at the same time. Here plays the feel-good theme song for the movie of my own life, "I Love Music" by the O'Jays. Disco drums and funky bass percolate as frozen farmlands sprawl.

I miss Annie in the way grass misses rain once snow piles up. A stream-of-consciousness winter survival list unrolls.

Bakery. Peppermint tea. Grape soda. Scratch-offs in holiday cards. Soup inventions. One-way jokeversations with Gerald the aluminum flamingo. Aretha. Flying Lotus. Ukrainian punk. Katy Perry in non-ironic ways. Music flowing out of the heat ducts. Music soft as a peach pie. Music louder than cops. Mousetrap drum solos on a spiral staircase. More music than there would be snow. These are the types of thoughts Wisconsin gives me.

I exit the freeway in Waukesha, the city where I grew up. Home is fifteen minutes away. It's the longest part of the whole drive. When I get there, Pops is waiting in the garage.

"Welcome home!" He waves.

Dad's retired. He built our brown-and-yellow three-bedroom ranch on one acre of land in 1976. Now he calls it *The Kingdom*. An American flag hangs, unwavering on a sullen pole where the basketball hoop once stood. I inhale decades of smells in one breath. Here sits root of the root. Home. Ground zero. Square one. The Keebler tree of my formative years.

When the house was being constructed, Dad brought me to see its empty frame. He gave me a hammer and I nailed scraps of wood in the studs at random. There was no ceiling. No roof. I looked right up through the house to the sky. It was a cloudy day. All the seventies were.

Inside, Sinatra sings from a radio near the pantry. The carpet zaps static shocks to the sock. A white-and-gold Bible leans against the king's recliner. *The Andy Griffith Show* is on TV in black and white. I put my stuff on the floor by the table. The kitchen boasts a fresh bouquet of cleaning chemicals.

"Gotta keep a house shipshape," Dad says. "Would you like tea?"

"If you have peppermint."

"What room are you sleeping in tonight? Upstairs?"

"Downstairs."

"It's warmer upstairs."

"Yes, but hearing the train in the night is hard for me."

He pauses. His face softens. The heat blows on, consoling the awkward silence.

"You'll sleep well down there. I put new winter sheets on the bed. Make sure you open the vent; it gets cold down there."

"Thanks, Dad."

The gray November sky does nothing to fill this house with light. The tea is sweet and quiets my mind and heats my throat. It's easy to be home. But there is a heaviness.

Losing Mom feels made up. A fever dream. I focus on the good. There was still lots of it in Dad's world. He tells me the Thanksgiving plan. We'd eat across town at Lois's house. Deep breath. Lois is not a replacement for Mom, but someone my dad can share life with. Don't push away from life what is loving and kind. Furthermore, she is funny and welcoming and understanding and her own happy person. Lois is a mother, too. I drove all this way for Thanksgiving, and plan on enjoying myself. Mom is everywhere, like air. Exhale. Anxiety exits the body.

I bring my bags downstairs. Two walls of the room are cinder block, one is plaster, the other paneling. A popcorn ceiling creates a white cave.

On the desk is my eighties stereo from high school and a family portrait in a bent plastic frame. A bookshelf holds Camus, Toni Morrison, and sheet music for the Top 100 Pop Hits of 1986–87. Even though the waterbed has been taken away, the room still smells of virginity and retainer cases.

At night, earplugs make it impossible to hear the monster train. But it is always near. A thing so loud, it rings in my skull even when not passing a mile and half down the highway. A devilish bullet of rust and steel. A wheeled beast.

Behind her gentle way, my mother harbored a hidden malaise. Her sorrow never leaves my side, but her beauty is alive in everything I see. She waged a war a for sixty-eight years. Those are epic odds. She did a five-star job of fighting what science never got sorted out in time. This woman was not weak, or lost, or ungrateful, or without God. Mom was a warrior. What led to the train was her business.

The next day we visit the Public Museum. Milwaukee is a twenty-minute drive from Waukesha. It was all farms and fields when I was a kid in the eighties. Miles of marsh and bog. But corporate chains invaded over time and built up a homogenized web between them. A matrix of parking lots and fast food now smothers once grassy acres as we drive.

"They got the Public Museum done up pretty nice now," Dad says.

"Well, I hope they haven't changed it too much. I enjoy the memories."

"Just enough."

We pass through the neighborhood where he grew up.

"Is this the hill you rolled my uncle down in a tire?"

"Until he hit the brick wall of the old Tannery. That stopped him."

The Tannery is condos now. He shows me other changed locations.

"That used to be an old filling station. Over there was a slaughterhouse. Today, it's all condos."

I watch the shadows move across his face as we go under a bridge. I see softness around the eyes, calm in the lines. Time has been kind.

"Who would want to live in a condo converted from a slaughterhouse?"

"Those people do. Over here was the interchange me and my dad took to Chicago for two-dollar steaks. Best steaks I ever had."

"What did you listen to in the car?"

"If the radio worked, Sinatra. That old car always had a loud hum going somewhere." He makes a buzzing sound with pressed lips. "Every once in a while he'd turn a polka on."

"Polllllkaholic!"

"That's right. Polka music is good music, and good music keeps people happy. We've even seen polka in Minneapolis together, buddy."

We park in a ramp under the museum, back to visit the mysterious taxidermy of our field trips. Stuffed bears and seals and turtles and birds nesting in plaster habitats. Around every diorama, school days sing.

My animal pals, you do not age. You are looking well. But as I pass the Great North American West exhibit, I note a condescending opinion in the rattlesnake's eyes.

The mummies on floor three are smug, too. We'd had such great imaginary times together. Twenty-five years isn't so long for a mummy. But they are bitter and old and say nothing about my returning.

Dad sits on a bench near an exhibit of Old Milwaukee before we leave.

"Are your knees sore?"

"Everything's sore. I'm old, kid."

Driving home through a sunless Milwaukee where there is no Mom. Passing pizza places where her laugh lingers. Nothing needs to be spoken. Her absence whispers about the breeze, not as a ghost, but a memory of a fuller world. There are two versions of me, before and after Mom. The reason it's called a nuclear family is because when one goes missing the results are atomic.

We make ice cream sundaes before bedtime because we hate to sleep soundly. I wonder if there's people who pray before dessert?

"Use these Dutch shortbreads," Dad says. "This is the good stuff."

"What? From Holland?" I scoop ice cream into a mixing bowl.

"From Aldi. Here's some hot fudge. You want nuts? They're under the counter. Pour a bunch on."

A sundae is a salad with better ingredients. Dessert before bedtime softens the struggles of the day. I've also read sugar causes nightmares. What do nightmares soften? Is it the brain fixing the mind? My father's whole career was fixing things at the plant. I wonder if he knows how to fix a broken life?

"Dad, once you told me, when fixing an engine, you picture yourself standing inside. Then you look around for the problem."

"Like you're a part of that machine."

"Is the same true with a personal crisis?"

"Absolutely."

"Let's pick something small." I plop a final heap of Moose Tracks from the carton into my bowl. "A scoop of ice cream falls off a cone."

"That's a big crisis. Are you kidding me?"

"Asking why it fell doesn't change the outcome. Crying at the ice cream as it melts on the ground won't make it reappear on the cone. There is no way to fix the problem. The only solution is a new scoop."

"What about if every time I got an ice cream, you knock it off my cone? Then the cause is the problem. Everything has two solutions, always remember."

"Always?"

"No." His face goes still. "Some things you can't fix. Some things you cannot change."

"I see."

"After your mom died, I had three dreams in the same night. In one I was repairing a furnace. My boss said, 'This furnace can't be fixed, it's done. John, it's beyond repair.' In the second dream, I was with your grandpa. We were working on his tractor. He was underneath, and he said to me, 'You can't fix it anymore. It can't be fixed.'" Dad pauses, swirling ice cream around in his mouth, lost in thought. "There's a third one, but I forget how it goes."

"I wonder what it was?"

"The same thing. Let go of what you can't fix."

I nod my head.

"But the one I'll never figure out is where she kept telling me about *A Midsummer Night's Dream*. 'Go see *A Midsummer Night's Dream* by Shakespeare.' I'm trying to figure out why. I read it. You and I even saw it together, Mark. All I got from it is that life is like a joke. Relax. Take it easy. Enjoy."

A soft house surrounds. Her spirit permeates every-thing, even cracks in tea cups. Our emotions mix together with the melting sundaes.

"Mark, I'll tell you, I've had some unbelievable desserts in my time. Rhubarb pie. Double chocolate cake with coffee in it. Tiramisu. And lots of ice cream. I loved it as a kid and I love it now. Mom would go to McDonald's and get that little cone she loved. It gave her happiness."

He slurps the last bits of goodness and says, "Ehhh, think I'm going to bed. Good night, buddy."

Dad rinses out his bowl and walks down the hall to his room. I move to the couch.

This sundae will take three hours of dedicated eating to finish. I surf TV till my pants don't fit. That day I'd eaten two butter burgers, half a bag of Wisconsin cheese curds, four peanut butter chocolate candy cookies, an elephant ear from a gas station with a bakery, a wet Italian beef sandwich with sweet peppers, and a Dr. Pepper float. I'm pregaming Thanksgiving.

I head to the basement chamber and pop some earplugs in. The sundae pushes my innards too close to the edge, just like the album of the same name by Yes. I lie in bed. A swift heat wraps my body, then a chill. I pass out into a food coma.

Morning comes. Without Mom, it isn't Thanksgiving but some new holiday with the same name. We watch TV in the afternoon, then drive to Lois's house. Dinner includes two cousins and their kid, Dad's second cousin, a surrogate boyfriend, one cop uncle, one divorced aunt, a priest whose brother recently died, a great-uncle from the days of cheddar cheese on apple pie, six other people I can't say I'd met before but who knew me by name, Dad, Lois, and me. It is loving and good, except for the cheese on the pie.

This is the third Thanksgiving since Mom died. The crisis is over but the loss lingers. I stare into the darkness looking for beauty. There is a reason for sadness, but I don't know what it is.

Dad knows because dads know everything. Here is a man who serves funerals at church, even for people he doesn't know. He once bought a hundred dollars' worth of jelly beans. He never swears around children unless they are his own. He invented the Egg Pancake, which is all break-fasts fried together in one Jackson Pollock painting of pan-cake batter and meat. He does not drink hard alcohol but took shots of brandy with me after Mom died. Three nights it lasted. Dad, who "made a promise to your mom, and made a promise to God." Who's friends with the priest, yet worries about getting into heaven. Who believes in angels. Whose nickname at the coffee shop is Oatmeal John.

When we get back home, he puts Sting Radio on. "Fields of Gold" plays.

"This is my favorite Sting song," I say.

"God, it's beautiful music." He sings along, more a gentle growl than anything. The melody is implied.

"You know all the lyrics?" I was impressed. "I've heard it hundreds of times at the grocery store, but I never paid attention to what it's actually about."

"It's about his girlfriend, when he first meets her, and she decides to take him outside and screw him."

"Right there in the fields of gold?" I laugh. "It's a dirty song!"

"I think it's a wonderful song. In the end, they have kids."

I go to the kitchen and heat up tea. Dad sits in the recliner next to a Bible. He breathes in deep through his nose.

"Music could be a smell to me," he says. "Every so often when I smell damp canvas, it reminds me of a 1953 Chevy convertible. That was my first car. Songs bring me back that same way. Those were good times."

"What songs remind you of good times?"

"It's got to have a beat and words that fit the beat. When I ran marathons, those songs helped. Roy Orbison had some good music, too."

"Well, I wouldn't play Roy Orbison to get happy."

I lie with my feet on the couch because I am an adult now.

"But when you're depressed, you look for music that fits."

"Do you think it helps?"

"No, I don't."

He blows on his tea.

"Well, if I'm in the dark, I put on happy music," I say. "Darkness doesn't serve me anymore."

"Buy some more lights. Mark, you have to go to Goodwill. Two, three bucks you can buy a lamp."

"I meant when I'm feeling dark inside. Emotionally."

He is insistent about the lamps.

"LED lights help."

"Hey, I put an LED bulb in the lamp you made me,"

He'd made a lamp out of an old bowling pin for my birthday. I keep it in my studio. It's never been shut off. Even now, 250 miles away, his lamp shines.

"I'm going to hit the hay, kiddo." Dad makes grandpa noises upon standing. "Don't get old, Mark."

I lie on the couch. Moonlight shines on the piano through the doorway. On top are photos of my brother's wedding, Mom and Dad's wedding, family reunions, Mom and me singing on stage, and me alone in a frame. In the center of these is the pink and amber ceramic urn. Mom. Her body condensed into a jar.

In the morning Dad cooks me breakfast. I bring up my stuff from the basement. We say our "I love yous" in the garage, and I drive back up to Minneapolis.

Then come many fabulous days in a row. I wake up without an alarm and go to bed whenever. Compositions come easily. It is more fun to write songs out of the house. There is an excellent view of the river from the yellow glass top of the Guthrie Theater and a bench to sit and write on. I see hand-holding couples in coffee shops who do not quarrel. I hear the varying stages of meeting and being in love. I write about trees with secret, intercoursing roots that grow together underground. I write about crows who mate for life. Turn the page.

This time of year, Minneapolis is vibrant and proud with colorful lights. A person could be convinced Christmas was invented here. As the cold comes, stillness is magnified.

There are days when I listen to no music at all. There are others when I park behind the garage and cry for no reason. This lasts the length of "Genesis" by Grimes. I remind myself that crying for no reason is OK. Employees in onion ring factories do it every day. Fear dwindles. There is beauty in small things.

At night, I watch television through the windows of my neighbor.

December

In the kitchen, the wall calendar still reads November. I tear this page off. With a marker, I scribble a manifesto for the new month.

Goals:
Step outside one's self.
Watch good things unfold.
Enact change in third person.
Turn off autopilot.
Create your now.
Be the child.
Quiet the mind.
The music is its own reward.

There is a garage across town where Eugene records his music podcast. It is early afternoon. The bent gate is stuck in mud and has to be forced open. Plastic tarps hang from clotheslines. A bunch of shovels lean on a dirty pink child's slide. Things that were made to be inside are outside. I imagine the kitchen floor of the house is congested with lawn mower parts. To the left of me is a collapsed statue of a cherub emptying a vase. A homemade TARDIS has been placed over the entry to the garage. Inside the garage is an internet radio studio. Out from the TARDIS steps a human hulk. Eugene.

"Yo."

"I was beginning to worry I was in the wrong junkyard." I step over a broken lawn chair.

"Nope, this is where we record."

"Do you plan on murdering me at the end?" I ask.

He laughs.

"I'll take that as a yes."

There is a drum set in a corner and a mixing board in another. Electric guitars hang on the walls. Underneath them is the type of furniture sectional you'd find in a frat house. We sit at an octagonal poker table with microphones on miniature stands. The fragrance of stale beer wafts about the room.

"Mic level?"

"Vo-cal-Vo-cal-Vo-cal. Too loud?"

"It's good. Let's start."

Eugene sifts through handwritten pages torn from a spiral notebook.

"Your latest record is philosophizing on the nature of happiness?"

"Yes. Songs can be a recipe for joy and healing. They can also be a recipe for evil and disaster. The chord is the conscience of the lyric. If we sang 'Happy Birthday' over a minor chord, it would sound sarcastic and insincere."

"If life is difficult for whatever reason, then we can turn to music to experience joy? To come together?"

"I don't think there's a point in history of music dividing people, except putting parental warning stickers on albums or something."

"Is the way in which you're ruminating about happiness informed by your work as a musician?"

Eugene speaks more formally than I'm used to.

"At the moment, my war is getting out of bed in the morning," I say. "This is why I'm exploring the issue of happiness. There's a different war I'm fighting."

"The war of . . . ?"

"The war of the self."

He interrogates me next about a stage rant the previous summer. I'd gone off the rails discovering a numeric disparity between love and hate in Google results. Hate turns up 591,000,000 results. Love scores 6,940,000,000.

"That's ten times as many incidences of love over hate. Yet we're biased toward our fears when we look at the overall scope of the world."

"We create our own heaven and hell, so to speak."

"That's where music's potency can steer the mind. For instance, Pharrell's 'Happy.' It's medicinal. It makes me happy. It also annoys people."

"Is this because of feeling the vibrations, feeling music in the blood as a life force?"

"I don't know; you'd have to ask Nikola Tesla that question."

We speak for over an hour. Before leaving, I ask Eugene about his bowling game. Earlier in the year I'd mentored him, and doubled his score with my radical teachings. Don't close your eyes. He bowled an 80.

"Haven't been since we went."

"Well, let's change that."

"Right on."

On the drive home, I stop to check the tire pressure. Two cars escape a slow crash in the parking lot. Everybody is a horrible driver.

I put on the Blind Boys of Alabama, "Run On for a Long Time." Seeing the Blind Boys at SXSW was powerful. Something about gospel when it's true rings deeper than happiness. When a magician reveals the trick, the magic dies. There's no trick to spirituality. All that's left is magic.

Not long ago, in summer, Dad and I made the hour drive from town to visit Franconia Sculpture Park. Dragonflies overtook fields between steel towers that swirled. Deep in the garden, past the boom-box tower and the house that looks like a dog, we found a sculpture called *Death Bed*. It was three stacked coffins. The top coffin was person sized, and each coffin increased in size beneath it. A stairway led to the top. I asked him to take a picture of me lying down on it. All I saw above me was Dad, the camera, and a cloudless heaven.

"It's a bit morbid, don't you think?"

"What is?" He snapped the shot and handed me back my phone.

"A death sculpture in a lovely park. On this lucky day."

"It's only morbid because you've been told to believe it's morbid. Death is part of life."

Dads are teachers who never retire. I took his old-man hand and helped him to the ground. We spent that afternoon with weird art, soft prairie, and industrious bugs. I'd live that day on a loop.

He calls as I exit the gas station.

"Hi, Dad."

"You sleep OK last night?"

"After my tea. Some bad dreams, though."

"Everyone has bad dreams, Mark. Think of the brain as a ball, spinning inside your head. There's a needle."

"A needle?"

"A record player needle. It taps, picking up different scenes as you sleep. You wake up in the morning and say, 'What the hell was all that?'"

"A record player, I like it. Once I dreamed there was of slice of pecan pie in place of the sun."

"You have good dreams as well, see? When I was about seventeen, I dreamed I bought a Ford Thunderbird. It was so real I had to look out the window in the morning to see if it was still there."

We continue to talk dream stories and Thunderbirds. Then Dad goes on a tangent about Beatrix Potter. He says she'd faced constant rejection at first and I should never give up on my dreams.

"Now she sells a book every fifteen minutes. Too bad she can't use the money."

"I've pretty much achieved a version of my dreams, but I already feel one hundred years old."

"Trust me, when you're one hundred, you'll know it. What are you going to do today? It's too cold for me to do anything, but you should. Be around people. It's good for you."

"You're right. I'll make a plan. I love you, Dad."

"Love you too, buddy."

We hang up. "I love you" keeps me on course. It's the last thing I ever said to Mom. The next afternoon, a horror roared through Waukesha, Wisconsin, one and a half miles from home. I didn't find out until that evening. It was the worst night on Earth. Always say "I love you."

Going with Dad's advice, I get a plan going. In the kitchen, my cupboards look less empty in the half light. I do what I do worst, cooking. My warped reflection in the slow cooker resembles that of a drunk tree.

There is just enough random unopened food for me to play the Dr. Frankenstein of soups. I pour half a box of chicken stock into the crock. Some vegetables are wilting on the bottom of the crisper. I put those in. There aren't any noodles or rice to make it thick so I use oatmeal. Yes, that's wrong. But it's the half jar of spaghetti sauce that puts me on tilt. What happens next is a food failure so severe, if Dad found out he'd disown me. Peanut butter. I open the jar and scoop the last gobs in. Regrets, I have a few. Nobody has ever died from awful soup, but part of my soul does. And that's the story of how Peanut Butter and Spaghetti Sauce Soup is invented.

"What have I become?" Desperate soups, desperate measures.

All we can do is work to be our best. To float through the alligator-infested swamp of life without sinking. Success is messy but we shouldn't let it stop us from jumping off the roof into a swimming pool fully clothed. Don't be afraid to get your pants wet.

Before bedtime, I clean off the countertop in shame and let the gruel brew overnight.

I wake up late for my sleep study evaluation the next morning. The kitchen smells like a Reese's Peanut Butter Calzone. I'm not in a hurry to taste this soup. I switch the crock to simmer. I still have yesterday's clothes on. It saves me time getting to the hospital. Didn't Einstein use this technique?

I'm late but the doctor still sees me. According to the polysomnography report, my sleep architecture is fragmented. This is due to an increased frequency of periodic limb movements (PLMs). The total recording time of the polysomnogram is 379.1 minutes. The sleep time was 242.0 minutes. There were 331 PLMs during the entire study, with an index of 85.6 movements per hour. The PLM arousal index was 17.1 per hour. Abnormal sleep-related behaviors are not noted. Also, there was clenching of the jaw. The doc recommends something called a "regular sleep schedule." He also says I should avoid sleep deprivation, get a mouthguard, and try pharmacologic therapy.

"Sleep drugs?"

"Gabapentin or dopaminergic agents could be considered."

"What are the possible side effects?"

"Impulsiveness. Depression."

Impulsive Depression has to be the name of a metal band somewhere.

"I'll think about it. Could the limb movements be from bad dreams? The nurse said it was like I was running in my sleep."

"If you'd like to try the Gabapentin, let the nurse know and I'll have her write a prescription."

We talk a bit more about anxiety and the brain. I turn down the medication.

The seven-page report is all I need. Here is some substantial research and proof that I am healthier than my fears suggest. I roll up the report and smack it on my knee.

"Do I get to keep this?"

"Yes. It's yours. Have a good day, Mr. Mallman."

This guy doesn't seem to have a concrete answer about my weird sleep. It is time to see a dream doctor, but I don't think my policy covers those.

In the parking ramp I reread the report. There is a cluster of graphs on page seven. Five instances of "night running" are followed by a spike in heart rate. After the spike, I wake up. Who am I running from? Cops? Piano teachers?

When I come home, I face the terrible soup. It's not fair to ingredients to be prepared this way. I've set the food world back 1,000 years. No one must know. I dump some scoops in plastic containers and hide them in the freezer under frozen okra that I'll never eat.

Over the weekend a snowstorm hits. Traffic trudges Cedar Avenue through coal-gray pudding. The temperature is dropping steadily. It's expected to be nineteen below zero by eleven. My holiday concert is a bull's-eye on the city's first subzero freeze. The show is called *Peace on Earth*. The band and I have been prepping for months.

"Darn it," I snap. In Minnesotan, that's swearing.

Notions of road hide under dodgy patches of black ice. The van slides across town in a 4 p.m. midnight.

Inside the club, staff is busy with opening preps. My light guy Tap Kit Johnny crows at me from a ladder. He's worked for me for fourteen years. His nickname is Tap Kit because once he tapped into city electric wires of the Triple Rock Social Club parking lot to jump-start his jeep.

"Any big surprises tonight, Mallman?"

"Depends on if I order dinner from the bar."

I fake high-five him from the floor. On the way to the dressing room I swing by the office. The owner is at his desk.

"Think the cold weather is going to hurt attendance?"

"C'mon, Mallman, it's Minnesota. Last night we had a great crowd. I'm not worried. People are used to this."

Positivity is contagious. My jackets, boots, and Santa suit are safe in the dressing room. I set up my piano side stage. Once Johnny's lights are focused, we bolt across the street to the Bad Waitress diner.

I know the night manager. We attended a monster truck rally ten years ago. She had a Mohawk then.

"I'm doing a show at Icehouse tonight," I say. "It's called the *Peace on Earth* show. Shall I put you on the list?"

"I have a date tonight. But I'll ask her if she wants to."

I order a glass of milk and a pancake. She rings me up.

"Oh, I have to tell you this thing I read about rats."

"Yeah, what is it?"

"Did you know they enjoy being tickled?"

"Ha ha, I believe it."

"They emit a frequency inaudible to humans," I say. "Rats laugh!"

"I don't keep rats anymore. Sign, please." She hands me the credit card receipt. "Too much work, though, keeping rats."

Our meals arrive. My steamy pancake is bigger than this flat planet. I would sleep on pancakes if I could. Johnny is having french fries and french toast. Van Morrison comes on the CD jukebox, "And It Stoned Me."

"Hey," I say. "I got this song on my Happiness Playlist."

"Been loving it all my life, friend."

"What a cool idea, a love song for water. You ever been stoned from water?"

"Vividly high, mountain hiking in Colorado. I was worn down. Short of breath. One drink of water, and it stoned me." He speaks through a mouth of fries. "Also, there's a swamp where I grew up, it's called a city park, but it's a swamp. We'd bike through the woods and light newspapers on fire. To this day, the smell of burning paper brings it all back. Unprovoked. Instantly to the front of my mind."

"What does that have to do with water?"

"It doesn't. But "And It Stoned Me" is a song as much about memories as it is about water."

The temperature is negative eight degrees by the time dinner is over.

Next, it's showtime. I'm a rock janitor late for work. *Peace on Earth* is a paid dress rehearsal. People have made it out despite the storm. Music friends get on stage to make the night special. Jess joins me on "Imagine." Hearts burst out through chest cavities. Maurice, as Santa Claus, convulses in caveman struts and shimmies. With each divine undulation, the set grows nearer to a close. I fall to the wall, wet with sweat. Streaks of hot lightning surge in my blood. If rock is dead, I've found heaven. How can anything be dead if it exists all around me? Music changes form. Mom did. Dad talks about animals in the woods, decaying into the soil, and becoming something new. Songs end. Shows end. Nights end. But they live forever in our stories. They live forever in songs. The show ends with a spaced-out version of "Silent Night" replaced with the words "Peace on Earth."

Outside, ice spaghetti covers everything. The band loads out. Magical Minneapolis is a white pearl.

Then comes sleep.

Deep oceans.

Memories.

I am five. Mom is eternal. Happiness swirls around us on the double-decker carousel at Marriott's Great America in Gurnee, Illinois. We can see the whole park lit up. It is the last ride of the night. A topaz fountain glows beneath. Roller coasters speed and twist up from the horizon of a carnival continent. It reflects in our firework eyes.

When winter is frightening, I ask, "Are the trees dead?"

"No, they're just sleeping." She tucks me in.

"What about the grass, Mama?" I ask again.

"The grass is also sleeping. Now it's your turn. Goodnight, dear."

"Goodnight, Mama. I love you."

"I love you, too."

But the city never sleeps, and the city never dies, and the end is not the end. When Mom was much younger than I am now, we played piano side by side.

"Everything is possible," she would say.

Tuesday morning. The temperature jumps sixty degrees in sixty hours' time. Sunday it was twenty-four below zero; today it's thirty-four degrees above. Maurice texts. He wants a ride to the DMV for his driver's test. The man is thirty.

"You need to make an appointment," I reply. "Six months in advance. That's what I did twenty-seven years ago, when I was sixteen."

"Not if we go out to Eagan. The Eagan DMV has a walk-in road course."

"We?"

"C'mon, man. I'm going to take the test in my cat costume."

This I had to see. I put on "Mr. Blue Sky" and drive into Uptown. Maurice strolls out, no costume.

"Hey now, buddy, I said I'd take you if you wore the cat costume." I shake my head. We laugh. I hit the gas.

The Eagan DMV is a multi-acre facility surrounded by a chain-link fence and small buildings that seem to be abandoned. A stakeout. In back sit two barren city blocks. The road course is a houseless neighborhood of stop signs, bent street lamps, and roads that go nowhere.

DMV employees drink coffee and chuckle back and forth behind a drive-thru window. A lady says, "I'm going to need his paperwork," pointing at Maurice with a Styrofoam cup. "And I'm going to need proof of insurance from you, too." She motions again with the coffee cup.

"Me? I already know how to drive."

The lady grimaces. She nods toward Maurice, eyebrows raised.

"I know how to drive!" he insists. None of us believe him.

"Well, if he's going to drive your vehicle, I need proof of insurance from you."

"My vehicle?" I turn to Maurice and raise my eyebrows.

"Hey, man, I didn't know."

I hand over my insurance card. She waves us forward. The drive-thru widens into five lanes. Each has a number at the end. I put it in park.

"The windshield fluid is this button," I say. "The rest is up to you. Godspeed."

A tester knocks on my door. I get out. Maurice jumps in my spot. The tester gets in Maurice's. Across the parking lot full of taxis, I walk to an empty waiting room with two vending machines.

Thirty minutes later, I am sprawled out, sleeping on a wooden bench. Maurice's howling startles me awake.

"Mallman, I passed! I gotta go back and fill out some forms. Then we can go. How's my hair look?"

"Let me fix it." After a few tosses of his unwashed hair with my unwashed hands, he is a drummer/rapper again. He should have worn the cat costume.

Maurice does his photo shoot and we dart.

On the drive into Minneapolis, strawberry vapor blows from his e-cig. I suggest we keep the windows cracked. Straggling snowflakes bounce along the interstate to the beat of The Happiness Playlist.

That night, I dream I'm waiting in heaven to see God or Buddha or Vishnu or somebody. Whoever he is, he's wearing a black suit.

"To be honest," He says, "I don't know how any of this happened. I'm just going along with it."

Before I get to reply, I'm hurried away by a bunch of guys in white suits. As we leave the room, I hear God say the same thing to the next guy in line.

December skips a beat. The weather is erratic. Dad calls. I invite him to town for Christmas, but there's impending weather. I-94 can be dangerous. Black ice. Drifting.

"I understand, buddy," I say. "Last night, I slipped in a parking lot. Twisted my ankle."

"Dammit, that hurts."

"It's fine. I put frozen vegetables on it. Hey, Dad?"

"Yeah?"

"I don't think I'll make it to Wisconsin either. Is that OK?"

"It's a bad road this time of year. We'll come up there when the weather clears up."

After the call, I head to my studio. It is a modest workspace compared to my peers'. Shelves are stacked with mixers and drum machines. There are bins filled with cables, microphones, harmonicas in every key, guitar slides, tambourines, and the life-size animal head of a plastic black panther. Two towering speakers meet the drop ceiling. On the wall hangs a velvet Elvis painting that could be mistaken for a velvet Nicolas Cage.

Next to my digital piano is a pencil to remind me where to begin.

The guitar amp is held together with duct tape. Give me raw over clever, candid over coy, authentic over snark. Give me a series of wrong notes in the right order. Chopin is fine, but nothing delights like the dissonance of a Frye boot on piano keys. Give me the pounding of fists on fake plastic ivory. Play me the sacred rumbles of grand pianos dropped from skyscrapers.

I have a bright-blue microphone cable used by Prince on the Emancipation tour. I record all my vocals through this cable. Anything Prince touched is holy.

My phone buzzes. It is a text from Annie. I smile.

"Work sucks today. How are you?"

"I'm in my studio. I'm working on a happy song, but it's mostly happy noise at this point."

"Noise? Well, that's nice. Ha ha."

"It makes me smile. What song makes you most happy?"

"I don't know."

"There's not a song anywhere that you play which makes you feel great?"

"Rap songs," Annie texts. "Like the 'oh yeah I want to party!' kind of happy."

"So when you play rap at the office, you're partying?"

"Yes, especially 2 Chainz. I love him."

"Say I put a burrito in a plastic cup of water for an hour. Would you drink the water, if you got to take winter vacation with 2 Chainz?"

"Yes."

"Noted."

I return to recording. The dry-erase board above me reads "Be Fire!" A collage of personal photos from studios, hotel rooms, backstages, and gas stations is pinned over my keyboard. A framed printout of the words "Live Below Your Means" hangs at the back of the room. Music has taught me to be esoteric often. Don't mistake babbling for genius. Smile imperviously. No job's as complex as they make it sound. Improvisation is elemental. Artists see opportunity where others see mistakes. In spite of his deafness, Beethoven thrived. Never aspire to anything. Be it.

Happy music is coming out of me. The playlist has seeped into my neuropathways. After hours of this intoxicating ritual, I am overstuffed with sound. A harmonious explosion sweeps over my body. Fingers pressing on eggshell keys, cracking in time. Sweet release. Bones contort, my body falls apart. It is bedtime. The next morning I wake up and repeat the ritual. It feels great.

Days later, it's Christmas Eve. I've stayed in Minneapolis for the holiday. For gobs of people, this day is just another Saturday in the world. I drive to the cookie store (gas station) for treats. The cashier gives me a blank stare when I joke about working in a gas station called Holiday on a holiday.

"Happy Holllliday!" I sing. She hates me.

The cookies are all eaten by the time I'm home.

Dad and I catch up on the phone. He and Lois make a plan to drive up shortly after Christmas. I am thrilled. Annie also texts. This thrills me too. It's not so bad to be alone here. The silent night is calming.

The mood is ripe for a holiday movie. I crack open a grape soda and watch *The Wizard of Oz* because *Die Hard 2* is terrible. Dorothy is singing "Over the Rainbow." Toto keeps looking off screen, instead of at her. A movie dog doesn't know that it's in a movie. The scene chokes me up. Because of the song, and also because of Toto. Dogs are innocent and true.

Mom, Dad, and I flew to Florida on Christmas in my teens. My brother was stationed at an Air Force base in Pensacola. We'd come to celebrate as a family. It was a cold December and the beach behind our hotel was barren. Everybody stayed inside. The lounge at this place was where I'd perform my first song in a bar. It was a Bob Seger tune. I'm certain I got the words wrong but I was a fourteen-year-old in a bar. There was carpeting on the walls. Mom and Dad danced together as I sang. I wish I'd played "Free Money" by Patti Smith. But I hadn't heard it yet.

During the day, it was thirty degrees. Record cold. On that lonesome beachfront, a pelican wobbled as it stood. The bird was a feathered statue of a thing. We stared eye to eye, two foreigners in a cold war. I was a weird kid and didn't relate to the world around me.

As I walked farther, I heard the sound of eighties video games chirping behind a fence. I jumped it. There was a whole arcade in there. It was empty, but operational. This was a treasure to be discovered. For whatever reason, the arcade was locked to the public. I was trapped inside with glee. Without any quarters, I pretended to play. Suddenly a door rattled. A guy walked in behind the games. He yelled, "Hey!" It echoes in my thoughts today. I hopped the fence and sprinted away, kicking wet sand behind me.

When I came to the spot where the pelican stood, it lay sideways on the beach. The feathers blew backward revealing the flesh. The bird was dead. Only an hour earlier, we'd made contact. Its beak was open. What was it trying to say as it left this world? Do birds have last words? Ocean wind hissed. Waves looped up and down to my left. Everything became black and white.

Fifteen years later, my parents were again in Florida. Mom sent me a postcard of a pelican. "Dear Marky, The pelican on this card is like the ones we see on the beach. Your father and I are having a wonderful time together. I only wish you could be here, too. Love, Mom. XOXOXO"

A day later, I got a call from Dad.

"Your mom was attacked by a pelican and had to go to the hospital. She was feeding them and ran out of fish, but one of the bastards swooped and bit her in the hand."

"Oh no," I replied. "Will she be OK?"

"Yes. It wasn't anything but a nip. Mom is strong."

The pelican postcard is in a cardboard box somewhere. There's a metaphor in whatever we choose to see. I think about Tom Joad and the turtle. Knowing what I know now, if I don't chalk all this up to coincidence, I'd sleep even less than I already do.

Some days after Christmas, the weather has calmed. It's a spicy twenty-five degrees. Dad and Lois drive up to visit. They stay in a hotel by the airport, ten minutes away. I meet up with them and we drive to the Mall of America.

On a third-floor terrace, overlooking a roller coaster, Dad sees my worn shoes. I thought wearing black socks would hide the holes.

"We got to get you some winter boots, Mark. It's almost January."

"Nah, these shoes work. I don't go outside much."

"Look at those holes!" Lois chimes in. We all laugh.

I wear shoes with holes because I'm in denial of snow. My paychecks go to pizza and bowling, not winter necessities. Dad knows the struggle. He picks out some waterproof winter hiking boots. They have a high arch and good traction. It's a nice gift. We hug. I'm grateful for any reason to hug him.

On the drive back to the hotel, we talk about the neighbor's chicken coop, which Dad built.

"He loves those chickens," Lois says.

"Are you going to get some chickens, Dad?"

"Hell, no!"

"Why?"

"They'd crap all over everything. They already crapped all over my garage."

The next day, in St. Paul, we split two slices of cake three ways. One is turtle fudge, the other raspberry crème. The sugar races in my blood. Dad tells a work story.

"You want to know how to clean up a mercury spill?" he asks.

"Yes, I do."

"Pour liquid nitrogen on it and get a broom." He answers with raspberries in his mouth. Dad's art is solving. He once fixed my van by listening to the wheel spin over the phone.

We say goodbye in the hotel parking lot. Dad hands me a plastic bag holding a jar of cashews, coffee cake wrapped in foil, and a rubber chicken.

"I love you, Dad."

"I love you too, son."

They point the Jeep toward Wisconsin and zip away. Three days later, a package arrives at my door. Priority mail. It's a box from Dad. Inside, it's filled with cookies.

Darkness falls before dinner. I want to share cheap tacos

with Eugene, and drop by his spot. His is a place where you knock on the door, open it a little, and yell hello inside. Eugene will shout back from wherever he is and invite you in.

This night, he is splayed out across the living room couch, reading Fitzgerald. On top of the spinet piano, a frail pine tree wilts in a pot. The best way to describe the tree is frightened.

"Did you have a nice Christmas?" he asks.

"When I drink grape soda, it's always a party."

I walk over to his writing room. A futon is pulled out flat. Eugene writes lying down. The shelves are stacked wall to wall. Somewhere in there is signed copy of Dave Eggers's *A Heartbreaking Work of Staggering Genius*. There is also a copy of Jay-Z's *Empire State of Mind*, which the rapper inscribed: "To Eugene, looks like you made it!"

"How many books do you think you have? Five hundred?"

"Couple thousand."

"Whoa. How many have you read?"

Eugene sighs at my question. "There's kind of a pedantic story about that."

He closes Fitzgerald and joins me in the library.

"Umberto Eco had one of the largest private collections in the world when he lived in Milan. Friends asked if he'd read all the books and he'd say, 'They're for reference.' He's dead now."

Times are best when it is Eugene and me alone. He shows me the power of silence, yet both of us edge for the next word. We agree about parallel universes. We agree about love. We disagree they are the same thing.

"Grab your coat. It's cold. Let's go. Yummy tacos await."

El Taco Riendo is more crowded than when Ingrid and I went.

"I recently watched *The Wizard of Oz*," I say.

"I've seen it so many times, I can't remember."

"It makes me cry when Judy Garland sings 'Over the Rainbow.' The way Toto looks at Dorothy, then off screen. She breaks the fourth wall."

"What do you mean, she?"

"Toto is played by a female. Terry the dog. She carries the whole movie. Terry as Toto. She reminds us, by lacking the ability to be anything other than a dog on a soundstage, that Oz is Hollywood. The farm becomes a soundstage. The world is a movie set."

"You're right. But what about the song?"

"'Over the Rainbow' is a song of unrequited peace. She's singing about some sort of utopia. Heaven. Disneyland. Taco Riendo. It's somewhere, we know that much. Dorothy escapes into this world of color, Oz. There she learns that the rainbow is inside of her."

"Oz is a fever dream. A near-death experience. What's over the rainbow? You're already over the rainbow, Dorothy. In fact, you are the rainbow."

Eugene walks to the bathroom. Through the window, the snow globe of Central Avenue twinkles against a bleak shadow sky. It is so dark, even at 5:30 p.m., a person can't see a hundred Totos standing outside, begging for tacos.

Eugene returns to the table. "You know Martin Luther?"

"The theologian?"

"Yes. He was the first one in more than 1,500 years who said, 'You don't have to wait for heaven to have happiness.' Even though he was a manic depressive."

I point at the people waiting in line. "You only have to wait for tacos."

We bus our trays and buzz out into the glacial paradise.

Eugene continues. "Martin Luther recognized what Freud

called the superego. You don't have to be perfect to be happy. You don't have to go over the rainbow. He's saying you can be psychologically happy right now."

I'm happy with my friend and a full belly. At home, I play piano for many hours. Days go by. New Year's Eve sneaks up fast. I don't have any plans. On a whim I text Annie.

"Oops, I didn't make New Year's Eve plans."

"Me neither."

Where does fate begin and coincidence end? We get a pizza and watch a Beatles cover band. Then we ring it in over fried ice cream at Little Tijuana with ten other strangers. She sips free champagne from a plastic flute. Breaking Benjamin blares on the speakers. The TV's closed captioning reads "Fireworks over Chicago, what a beautiful sight." I am back at my place by 1:15. The breathing house smothers the ringing in my ears.

She texts, "Thank you for a perfect night."

"Likewise. Thank you, too!"

If your soul feels empty, try fried ice cream.

January

O n a twenty-first-century New Year's Day, the city is a freeze frame. Even the classic rock station doesn't play U2 anymore. Everybody is too hung over for wake-up sex, and for once, they make it to brunch on time. Twisted stir sticks are planted in snow banks. You see kids sledding by themselves. Cabbies sleep all day till dinner, then eat quietly, and go back to bed. Your father is somewhere joking with other seniors about writing last year on all their checks. Dogs have no clue that it's a new year. Flat champagne isn't mouthwash. I go to the computer and pull up Nico performing "The End" on a harmonium from 1974.

"Wait. Don't go down that pit. Quiet the mind."

I stop Nico, and put on "The Luckiest Guy on the Lower East Side" by The Magnetic Fields. I drink orange spice tea from an Abbey Road mug. My neighbor across the street is already taking Christmas lights down. He rolls up string lights around his arm. Then he stuffs them in a bag.

The phone rings. It's Jones. He is calling to tell me about a TV show.

"I watched this show about Harry Houdini, the magician. On it a woman woke up tied to a chair. Instead of panicking, she said, 'I know you won't hurt me, because I'm a psychic.' She was scared to death but used her brain to scare her kidnapper instead."

"In real life, a mind couldn't do that. The anxiety would be paralyzing."

"Not necessarily. In any situation, it's possible to take action."

"So, instead of being consumed by fear, she focused her energy on finding a way out? Where was Houdini through all of this? Couldn't he set her free or something?"

"I told you, she was kidnapped. Not by Houdini."

"Did you know what Harry Houdini's last words were?" I asked. "It was 'I'm tired of fighting.'"

"He had a mortal wound when he said that, Mark. He was tired of fighting the mortal wound, not life. Before the mortal wound, Harry was in a lot of situations where people would give up. His hands were bound. He was put into a box underwater. He'd say, 'I'm not going to be fearful, I'm going to find a way to get out of this,' and put his plan into action. Just 'cause your mind is worried, it doesn't mean give up."

"My mind worries most that I'm losing my mind."

"The mind is a concept. It usually refers to the higher functions of the brain. When you talk about losing your mind, you're talking about losing your higher functions."

"It's a valid fear."

He chuckles. "Houdini would say, fear is what our brain is cooking up. Worry is the problem, not your mind."

Jones insists that even if I do lose my mind, the lower portions of my brain will function. The lower parts of the brain are the most fun parts anyway.

We talk about upcoming gigs. I try to get him to press vinyl instead of CDs. Then we talk about Elvis.

When the call is over, I think about how neat it will be if Jones lives to be a hundred.

Before bed, I do an assignment from my therapist. It's to make a list of ten things I'm thankful for. The list starts with "Escapade" by Janet Jackson.

Then come my near record of good sleeps without nightmares. A snake dream breaks the trend. I imagine I'm in a boudoir of an ex-lover in New Orleans. She is dressing in a gilded mirror. I reach to hold her but she wears a pet snake around her neck. It bites my finger. According to a dream dictionary, a snake biting a hand suggests a preoccupation with a relationship that needs to be overcome. Annie?

It's time to venture out for music supplies. I walk to my subzero alleyscape of garbage and brown ice. The van is frosted. I flick on the rear wiper to clear a cracked ice sheet. It breaks up but the wiper gets caught. Crunch. The ice breaks away revealing the day. I tap the wiper again. More ice shatters. Something isn't right. I turn around for a better look. Oh no, that isn't ice. Somebody has shattered my back window in the night. Half of the window falls inside the van.

Behind me, glass shards sparkle on the driveway. The first worry to cross my mind is a squirrel or rabbit getting cut. I get a broom. As I sweep up my van window, I ruminate on assailants. A tiny meteorite? Someone training for a winter biathlon? A drunk eagle? Knowing sordid details of an accident doesn't undo the damage.

My neighbor steps out through our shared garage.

"That's from a bullet."

"No way."

"Looks like a pellet or a BB to me," she insists.

"A BB shattered the whole back window?"

My broom springs and bobs along the frozen pavement.

"Either that or a .22."

It is sad seeing hard-earned pieces of the band van glistening on the asphalt. One moment I am headed for guitar picks. The next I'm sweeping up glass. The soonest repair appointment won't be for days. I make a fake one with packing tape and cancel my plans.

During the week I'm contacted by a Hollywood friend about a music job. She's an actress and a psychic.

"I'm as much an actress as I am a psychic," she says. "And vice versa."

After catching up, I ask if she can give any recon from the beyond.

"Tonight, I'll channel."

Around midnight I get an email.

Mark,

I am just going to start channeling via writing. I don't filter anything. I will just write what comes through me, that feels pure, and then hit send. I don't claim to know any answers.

You are not alone, but sometimes your journey is. None of the energy is abandonment. I want you to know that you are about to change miraculously. Not this year, but sort of this year. Timing is meaningless when you can create time, which you can. Channel through songwriting. It is the raw, beautiful, sometimes painful truth from your spirit guides and ancestors.

Your life is several ancient dramas woven together, something about joyful saints and Renaissance artists. Hildegard von Bingen. Michelangelo. You are discovering uncharted human territories, like after St. John of the Cross came out of his dark night of the soul. I think you are a Renaissance person in the modern age. Please eat some extra onions and garlic and check in on liver-

and spleen-detoxifying foods because your system needs some extra support.

Oh, by the way, I am supposed to tell you to read Psalm 100 regularly. Plant the seed in your subconscious. It isn't a thought choice, but a swooping of music and light. Keep writing and playing music. Your mother is in a place, or going to a place, where it is all unconditional love and you do not need to worry.

Remember, you are part of a tapestry of love through storytelling, that is the best thing I can offer you. It's a done deal. The rest is joy.

White-noise tinnitus rushes out of my faucet brain. The sound of washing dishes. Strong breezes. Lips that shush the baby. Coming from somewhere beyond the drop ceiling is a swamp of a tune. Phoebe Bridgers's "Smoke Signals" plays from the computer upstairs. I follow the sound. How long had it been playing? Somewhere in the day, I was reading a music news story about the song and it repeated on a loop. This dark temptation is foiling my Happiness Playlist experiment. But I can't stop listening. It's beautiful. The music coaxes me to the living room where Bridgers sings about trash burning on the beach and living at a Holiday Inn.

If ever a Bleakness Playlist was created, it would only need this one song. Night deteriorates with every repeat. In the last lyric, she sings, "I am a concrete wall." The living room floods into a dead lake. The catharsis is complete. I shut off the speakers mid-lyric. Her voice loops about the house cloaked in tinnitus and silence. It seeps into the floorboards and stains my rugs. How do I explain to the landlord that his floor was soiled by a song? The mind clatters an array of fears. I shiver onto the patio.

"Get out of my head, Phoebe Bridgers," I whisper to the stars, breathing the wintry gloom. But the ear worm does not go away.

Is The Happiness Playlist permitting joy or prohibiting emotion? After Mom died, I couldn't bear to be alone. Driving, flying, even walking around the lake alone got scary. Thankfully, happy music stepped in. It holds me on the days I feel abandoned. But something in "Smoke Signals" tells me there's a deeper path than simple happiness.

When Annie moved on, I chose to be alone. I learned to be alone without being lonely. A fear of spiders is overcome by exposure to spiders. By avoiding them, the fear is reinforced. This is called progressive desensitization. I worked to return to lonesomeness. Movies, concerts, readings, museums, and restaurants were all places I relearned to enjoy by myself. The way over is through.

I go back inside and brush my teeth. Next, stirring in the brain, comes an idea. Give permission to sadness. Don't build a tower of isolation against your fear. Welcome in the sad song. Then, let it pass. I climb into bed, the Bridgers song looping on.

Is this the right choice? Will I spiral back to September 1, 2014? Will minutes later find me hiding under the bed again? It was a controlled burn, a small step toward calm, away from blind happiness. Baby steps aren't easy just because they are tiny. Ask a baby.

Comparable to saying a word over until it becomes a meaningless rhythm, Bridgers's melody repeats. It becomes a blanket, then a wall, then the air around me until it is gone. As much as I own my bed, I own my sadness.

Sometime in the night the speakers shut themselves off. In the morning, I wake up happy. Catharsis is a cleansing. I take a bath and text Annie.

"Good morning, Annie."

"Hi!"

"Would you ever take a bath in spaghetti?"

"Oh hell yeah. What about worms?"

"Candy gummy worms. Not sour. I would not take a bath in salsa."

The computer plays Sade, "By Your Side."

At lunch, Annie texts again. "Grape jelly?"

"Grape jelly wha?!"

"Would you take a bath in grape jelly?"

"Gah! Grape isn't even jelly. It's a scam. It's warm Jell-O."

"What would you take a bath in then?"

My best response is to send back the cover of Michael Jackson's *Dangerous* album.

Days edge onward. My bleached sweatpants hang low on the waist. A white flag. January slides by on hockey skates. I debate smoking Kools again. Classic pulp literature collects dust on the desk. My body becomes the couch's main appendage. Next, Lizzo's "Good As Hell" comes on. I bask in the power of underthinking things.

Pizza drivers of South Minneapolis are the sole humans I encounter. They peer with great suspicion inside my bongless residence. I wonder if anybody keeps a bong around for decoration purposes. When our promised utopia of drone-delivered pizza comes to fruition, the world will be that much lonelier. To avoid becoming hardened, I remember that. Life gets better with every pizza. Today's pie is green olive and pineapple. I set it on the table, open the box, and inhale deeply. Each breath of pizza steam fuses my body with the air. The basis of meditation is diaphragmatic breathing. Besides square breathing, alternate nostril breathing, and resistance breathing, there is pizza breathing. In this form of pranayama we achieve Zen through smell. Close the eyes. Release. Feel the tension move up from the socks and through the sweatpants. Release. Breathe in through the nose, hold the aroma, and release through the eyeball corners. Repeat this cycle until you are so relaxed you fall face first into the pizza. It is then that the two become one.

One day, a repair guy calls.

"Mark Mallman?"

"Yes. Hello."

"I'm here to fix your van."

I put on boots with no socks and a coat. Out back, a fellow in a parka climbs from a repair truck.

"Looks like you got shot out!"

"Shot out?!"

"Yep. This is a BB or pellet hole."

"How do you know?"

"Been doing this a long time. If it were any bigger, I'd have to find the casing. It's a legal thing."

Cold air blows through my sweats. "Yikes."

"Somebody mad at you?"

"No way. People like me. I'm fun." I rethink it. "I'm fun?"

"I'm kidding you. It's teenagers. They drive up the alley shooting at anything. I see it all the time. Been putting windows in for thirty years."

"Thirty years. You must be the window repair master."

"Never thought I'd end up doing this, but it's been good to me."

The guy walks around to the back of his truck for more tools. "Make sure you give this glue time to dry before you go driving around."

"Will do."

I hold my pants up through my coat pockets and walk back inside.

Windows shot with pellets in the silent night aren't loud

enough to wake us. When a person breaks, the shatter is un-
mistakable. Shards scatter on the carpeting below. Without
the glass, snow blows in where it's not supposed to. What a
nightmare when the outside comes in. When birds fly into
windows, neither can be fixed. Only one can be replaced, and
it's not the bird.

Nights later, I perform a concert. I hadn't played a Mon-
day in town for fifteen years, but this was special. It is the
night of the First Avenue staff party. We unload the van from
the street into the side of the club. The new rear window is so
clear that nobody notices.

It's problematic hauling 4-by-12 speaker cabinets over
ice. Guitars need to warm up before coming out of their cases.
My band doesn't soundcheck, just stages the frozen instruments. Afterward, the four of us head into the Main Room
where club staffers celebrate. They sing karaoke. Someone
has chosen "Killing in the Name" by Rage Against the Machine. Dissonance assaults the airwaves, making everything
hard to hear.

A woman approaches me between the second-floor bar
and the glass wall overlooking the stage. She's not a staff
member, most likely a guest.

"What do you do here?" Her eyes fail to blink, glaring
into mine.

"I don't work here. I'm a musician." I shout over the gnash-
ing sonic haze. Her face lights up. Not the typical response.

Her body brushes against me as she pulls herself closer. I
am being seduced. Wet heat fills my ear as her voice distorts
the drum inside.

"Do a trick for me."

"A trick?"

"Tricks are my favorite." Her hand moves down my
shoulder to my waist.

"I don't know any tricks."

"What kind of a magician are you then?"

I shake my head, playing an invisible piano with my hands on the table. "I'm a mu-si-cian." Her face becomes plain. We make small talk for a minute, then she is gone.

Legend goes the club is haunted. Ghost or not, she was certainly disappointed. Who goes to a nightclub to meet magicians? It takes all types, I suppose. As Roky Erickson says, "When you have ghosts, you have everything."

Silver trays of catered Thai food are lined up on tables. I make two trips. There are tens of pink donut boxes from Glam Doll Donuts. Coconut-iced caramel-drizzled toasted coconut rings, espresso cream cheese chocolate iced long johns, and bourbon-infused apple fritters with caramelized bacon. I make three trips. Of all the wonderful clubs in this town, First Avenue feels most like home.

Someone karaokes 4 Non Blondes while I tongue the frosting from my third donut. Then I return to the 7th Street Entry to prep for my show. Backstage is downstairs. It is a fluorescent-lit, gloss-black room. A dormitory refrigerator is stocked with tall boys. Torn-up leather couches are against each wall. One black. One brown. A framed mirror is hidden by band stickers. They read: *Ego Death. Blood Red Shoes. Rats and Children.* You never see stickers of famous bands in green rooms. I call this phenomenon "The Local Band Sticker Curse."

You'll find two types of people backstage: the band and not the band. A couple of fellows in puffy coats huddle over the table. This breed of drug-hungry, fashionably anti-establishment, bottom-feeding, socialite vampire are my least favorite. A shifty hush stirs about them.

"Want some, Mallman?" A guy holds out a rolled dollar bill, not making eye contact. Who is this guy?

I hold up a donut and say, "No thanks, I got this." It was safe to assume he wasn't offering me the dollar. That, I could use.

The ripped couch welcomes me to lie down instead. Not even my art school imagination is capable of conjuring what activities have taken place on this couch. I submit to rest, but give second thought on closing my eyes, considering the company.

Daydreams of a donut dominion jumble my brainscape. Bakery clouds roll in. Frosted fingernails stroke the cosmic curve of my french cruller. In caramelized crimes, whispers leak blueberry compote. I float in and out of a chocolate dream.

The first time Mom joined me in the 7th Street Entry was a total surprise. She and Dad had driven up for the show on a whim. I looked out over my piano, and there she was, dancing in the front row.

"I'd like to introduce to you my mother!" I howled. The packed room cheered. Fans assisted her onto the stage. She was in her late fifties at the time. Depending on how she controlled her voice, it could be as pure as Roy Orbison or as brash as Johnny Rotten. I could only aspire to command an audience like that woman. Mom was gifted. She drew her inspiration from visionary divas like Tina Turner, Cher, and Madonna. Through my mother, these artists became influences of mine. When I asked her how she did it, she said, "The more you keep singing, the better you'll get." It worked.

At twelve thirty in the morning, we hit the stage. I enter the trance. Johnny hammers on the lights.

We are inside a pinball machine. Power chords thunder. The floor-tom roars. Some celestial computer program is spitting words out of my head.

"Love dies! Love revives! Love thrives! Love waits!" I sing. The speaking in tongues bypasses my frontal lobe and becomes automatic. "Love dies! Love revives! Love thrives! Love waits!" It comes without premeditation. This eight-word cycle loops from the lips. Marathon-long performances have taught me how to slip in and out of music's grip. Inventing mantras, I bob up and down in a type of third-person point of view. It's an awareness similar to watching my own self driving from the back seat of a car. Love dies. Love revives. Love thrives. Love waits. I don't know what it means but it feels right.

Seventy-five minutes later, the chaos and creation is over. In the afterglow, I lean my forearm against the cinder block wall. Sweat drips off my forehead onto the floor. People are still hanging around. A young man approaches.

"I've never seen a singer get into it like you. Where does it come from?"

"Did you ever see the movie *Poltergeist*?"

"I believe it."

"Also, from my mom."

The band finishes load-out. I wave goodbye as a blast of winter between doorways boogies in my blood.

I met a woman who grew up in California. She told me she'd wondered as a girl what it would be like to have an ice cream cone that never melted. Her Minnesota winter fantasy was a January cone. As an adult she'd moved here and the dream became real. "I walked in the snow for miles but the ice cream never melted. It was magic."

January skates on. I spend as much of it as I can listening to The Happiness Playlist. Two nights in a row I have celebrity dreams. The first night, I ask Paul McCartney for his email address. He keeps writing it wrong.

"It's a very simple hotmail.com address," he says. Paul scribbles down half an email, crosses it out, then does the same again.

McCartney's manager scowls. "Paul, we got to roll out!"

A private jet appears. Paul is hurried away. I never get his email address.

The next night, I dream I'm looking out the window as toy paratroopers drop into the neighborhood. Dad grabs me by both shoulders. He insists I lend him the van.

"The president must get to his cousin's house before dinner," Dad said. "The state of America depends on it. Give me your keys, son. Your keys!"

They zoom out of the driveway. A shadow covers me. In the sky, a huge hamburger is being docked by a giant bottle of ketchup.

"We're being invaded! Save yourself!"

I don't worry about weird dreams. I'll worry when they get normal.

The following afternoon, while relaxing on the kitchen linoleum, I reflect on the sleep running. What if I take a nap right here on the floor? Will I start nap running? If I just daydream, will I only imagine I'm running? When will it end? My phone buzzes. It's Maurice.

"I leave for LA tomorrow. Want to grab slices?"

"Just ate soup, but I'll go," I reply. "Get this, last week a psychic told me my life is about to change."

"How?"

"In a swooping of music and light that could begin as early as February."

"Through which medium?"

"Clairvoyance."

I peel my body from the ground and drive to Maurice's. I inflate with each breath of January air.

He steps out his front door in a porkpie hat, unmatching scarf, and bent-wire sunglasses. Randy Newman's "You've Got a Friend in Me" is playing.

He gets in the van and whistles along. "That melody!"

"It sounds like a little dance." I wiggle my finger to the beat. "How old were you when *Toy Story* came out?"

"I watched it three times a day when I was eleven," Maurice says. "This song still makes me happy."

"It makes me happy, too."

Inside Mesa Pizza, Maurice orders a slice and two chocolate chip cookies. For me, nothing, but I'm eyeing his spare cookie.

"Are you packed for LA?" I ask.

"Hell, no," he says.

It'll be interesting to see how it unfolds for Maurice. A drummer/rapper gets to a point in a small city where the bigger gigs aren't available. Either you suck it up and get a side hustle, or upgrade to New York, Las Vegas, or Hollywood. Minneapolis isn't going to cut it if he wants to stay full time. Only the music gods know how it will unfold.

He finishes the pizza slice. I'm certain he'll split the two cookies between us. He doesn't. Who hogs cookies after singing "You've Got a Friend in Me"? I guess Maurice is ready for Hollywood after all.

We drive back to his place.

The temperature has become above freezing for a spell. Snow piles on corners are now deep gray from exhaust and malice.

Maurice rents a top-floor duplex. He shares it platonically with an internet dominatrix. This place is so old the wood floors creak without even stepping on them. The smell of incense sticks covers up the weed and cigarettes. In the main room, two soft light boxes hang for cam modeling online. There are acrylic platform boots and G-strings in piles. A green Flying V guitar leans against the ripped sofa. From his bedroom, Maurice brings a tarot deck.

"Let's go to the kitchen. I'm an optimistic reader. I see the good in bad cards. You can tell me how I stack up next to that clairvoyant who read you."

We sit in a windowed corner overlooking the yard. He lays the cards face up.

"What is that, a pentagram?" I ask. "Are these cards satanic, Maurice?"

"Pentagrams don't mean satanic."

"They do on Ozzy Osbourne albums."

"No, a pentagram stands for Earth."

Maurice shakes his head, flips the deck, and hands it to me to shuffle. I snatch the deck away.

"It's not Vegas, dude. Shuffle gently. And I'd suggest not bending them. When the deck feels ready, ask your question."

"If I eat brain tacos, will they make me smarter?"

"This is a meditative experience. Ask something to improve yourself."

Out the window, crows swing from trees on invisible swing sets. "Where is happiness? Am I doing life correctly?"

Maurice draws the cards and places them in a cross formation.

"A five-card spread."

They are Ace of Cups, Eight of Swords, Four of Swords reversed, Two of Swords, and Six of Pentagrams.

"This Eight of Swords represents the general theme of the present moment. You can see this person is bound up and tied. You've fought all these battles, yet you're stuck in the same swamp."

He moves his hand over the cards.

"This card over here is your past influences. You've been dumping out wealth, but the water is flowing back into the cup. What does it mean to you?"

"I don't know what any of this means."

"Let's move on to this Two of Swords card. You're hold-ing these swords, blindfolded. If somebody taps you on the shoulder, what are you going to do?"

"Ummm . . . ask, who is it?"

"Wrong. You're going to yank out that sword and slice!" Maurice whips through the air with a swish. "The other in-terpretation is, you need to make a choice. Each sword is powerful. No matter what choice you make, it will be OK."

"What is that number for?"

"I told you. It's a Two of Swords."

"We could totally play poker with these cards. Are there fifty-two cards in there?"

"Seventy Six in the Major Arcana."

"Well, we could play a hyped version of poker."

Refusing comment on my poker idea, Maurice clears his throat and gestures to the configuration.

"At the top is your potential," he says. "This is a morbid card when it's upright, but it's reversed. This whole spread is very financial."

"Is this the point where you ask me for money?"

Maurice just looks at me. It's safe to assume the reading is finished. He lights a cigarette and walks me to the door.

"I thought you quit?" He shakes his head, holding the door open. I leave. He says nothing. This is how we show each other love.

The next day, because of the tarot, money is on my mind. I go to my studio to find something to sell. Maurice has been bugging me to sell him an old drum machine, but he never has the money. Even if I cut him a deal, it's never enough. I think he wants me to give it to him. Maybe he should have split those cookies with me. I decide it'll never happen and box the instrument up. Always save the box.

It is a silent drive to the music shop. The owner is an exmetal guy. He's cut his hair and put his energy toward something more rewarding, dealing antique rotary phones on the side.

On the crowded front counter, underneath rows of guitar strings, sits a flame-orange landline.

"You should hear it ring. That phone has a bell inside. It's mechanical, not digital. Beyond analog sound right there. It's the store phone."

We stare at the phone. It doesn't ring.

In the nineties, this joint was all broken tubas and weird organs piled to the ceiling. If you needed an accordion, or a gong, or a beat-up trumpet, this was the best musical rummage sale around. Over time, he got sick of junk piling up. The store became only rock instruments. I'd bought my Wurlitzer piano, Rhodes piano, and Gibson 335 here. I've also sold things I'm too ashamed to admit. This drum machine wasn't anything special. Not to me.

"This machine is in good shape," he says. "I pay more for stuff that's been taken care of."

He writes some numbers on the back of a pink receipt book and flashes it to me.

"Yeah, that works."

"Cash?"

"Love it."

He goes to the back room to get payment. In this business, there's always a back room. Even though we aren't close, he and I have shared experiences. Mutual friends getting successful and moving away. Mutual friends becoming unsuccessful and moving back.

I browse the synths and guitars people have sold over the week. In a few minutes, mine will be here too. A shop proprietor has dirt on every instrument discarded. There are novels of letting go within this orphanage.

Together, we count the money on the glass counter.

"How are things?" he asks.

"Well, winter has certain emotions that come with it." He can sense what I'm getting at. He knows about Mom. He knows loss.

"You know, two years ago, my grandmother died." He hands me the money. "Then my good friend died. It's taken a long time to shake out of."

"How do you feel we fix ourselves when we are broken by these things?" I ask, tapping on a Farfisa organ.

"Every person has to trust intuition. It's never wrong."

Another customer comes in. I thank him and head out. Upon leaving, I hear the clangy chime of the plastic rotary phone. Its steely ring is a refreshing reminder of a time left behind. He gives me a knowing nod through the store window. I wonder if anybody plays rotary phones in a band.

I don't want a pretend life, to skip anguish, and never feel it. To accept I'm emotional is to accept the totality of feelings. When I think of Mom, joy and pain are inseparable. They come carpooling through my heart. There's grief with loss, but also strength and growth. Kindness flows inside. Under the skin. Between the blood.

In the van, I switch the radio on. The classical station plays a wondrous piece of melancholy piano music. It is "Nanu" by Chucho Valdés. The song feels like a massage, but it's not in line with my winter philosophy of happy music. Phoebe Bridgers's "Smoke Signals" was the exception. It taught me catharsis works, but my intuition says that's as far as I need to go for now.

I open up The Happiness Playlist. Velvet Underground's "Rock & Roll" begins. I turn it up. Lou Reed is talking that 1960s New York street rap. A smile forms. The corners of my mouth lift. Two wings. I am so happy, I drive with my knees.

Dad calls. He has to catch me up on recent grocery finds.

"I love a good deal, Mark. Blueberries for $2.99."

"I love blueberries."

"How's your morning, buddy?"

"Earlier, I was writing down parts of life that make me happy. It reminded me of the sign Mom made for your fortieth birthday surprise party. Remember, she had written out the lyrics to 'My Favorite Things'?"

"Yup. And then she'd listed all the stuff I liked. Your mother was good to me."

"What were those things?"

"Probably ice cream, kids, music, cars, and boats."

"Are they still your favorites?"

"There's been a lot of ice cream, I'll tell you that."

"What about the other stuff?"

"Oh, for sure. Especially music and boats. When I was a kid, I asked a lot of questions. My dad sent me to help recondition a boat called Cherry Queen. There were only five Cherry Queens ever made. This Norwegian shipbuilder, Norby, gave me the job of pounding dowels into the boat's new planks. I spent half that summer plugging these holes with dowels. One morning, Norby told me the wood grain on the plug wasn't matching the plank. He made me take them all out. I spent the next half of summer carefully lining them back up. The next day, Norby painted the Cherry Queen white. He went right over the perfect wood grain and all my work. I realized he made me take the dowels out so I wasn't standing next to him asking questions about boats all day."

"Norby!"

"So the end of the summer comes and I didn't get paid. Nothing. I guess he felt he was keeping me out of trouble or something, but that Cherry Queen was a fine-looking boat."

"Even painted white?"

"Even painted white. I don't regret it. I learned about boats that summer. Everything is yin and yang. Even if I could go back, I'd probably end up doing it the same. I was a kid."

It is a sad story that for whatever reason Dad thought was funny. Most of his funny stories are from this childhood period. His family struggled but they always had love.

"Is childhood the best time of life?"

"Middle age. That's the best time. You can see you're getting older, but you got your health. You're able to enjoy things. It's not all work. In middle age, the kids are grown, and it becomes more about you again. I believe we live in sevens. At seven years you're no more a child, you're a grown kid. Then you're a teenager. Next you're an adult. That area between twenty-one and thirty-five becomes your foundation for the rest of your life."

"What's the most difficult seven years?"

"I don't know. I haven't done them all yet."

Then we talk about grocery deals again. This goes on for a while. At the end we say "I love you."

On Saturday night, the Minnesota Zoo has an after-dark cocktail hour. It is called Adult Night. Annie gets us tickets in advance. We continue to be best friends. It's wonderful. There are no angry or jealous sentiments between us. We don't see our relationship as something that failed. Trying to force romantic love is like spitting on the ground and waiting for flowers to grow. Plus, we are too amped for Adult Night to question this fantastic friendship.

We drive against the grain of winter. Len is singing "Steal My Sunshine." Wind slaps the side of the van like jets.

"Look at that weird truck," says Annie. "I bet there's aliens in the trailer."

"I bet there's aliens driving, too. They're around us all the time."

"I'm an alien."

"From where?"

"Duh. We live in the same neighborhood. South Minneapolis."

"I'm aware. But where, originally?"

"St. Paul."

I pull the wheel against the wind to keep in my lane. "Do your parents know?"

"I don't think so. I was swapped at birth."

"Why aren't you on your home planet?"

"I like cheese and dogs. But I don't eat dogs. We don't have those."

"Some people eat dogs."

"I'm not a person."

It is impossible for either one of us to keep a straight face. Laughing with Annie stops time. I feel safe, even on blizzard roads. I offer her a stale curly fry from the floor of the van. She declines. Hard light sheds from chain restaurants and gas stations. The snow glows with cheap decadence amid a galactic flood of sameness. Same Chili's. Same Dollar Store. Same electronics outlet. Same Sim City architecture.

Adult Night at the zoo happens once a winter. It's a popular event. There is a line to park the van, and then a line at the entrance. There is a line for cocktails inside, and a line to see the seahorses. Minnesotans wear parkas over evening wear because there is a line for the coat check. Down the corridor, penguins are line-dancing behind glass. We make jokes about bands with animal names. A Flock of Seagulls. Eels. Sheryl Crow.

My favorite animal is the platypus, of which there are none in America. Dogs are Annie's favorite. But Gilligan isn't coming, so why are we here? I guess for the cocktails. I hadn't had a Shirley Temple in decades. Was it called something different now? A Honey Boo Boo?

"Spendy drinks, eh? I guess I'd rather give my money to a zoo than a bar," I say.

"Tonight, the zoo *is* a bar."

"But the money goes somewhere better than up the owner's nose."

"Animals are so great and we are such jerks."

The outside exhibits were closed, but there was much to explore. I put my arm around her. Fireworks light my melty heart. We debate animal hairstyles and multicellular organisms as international superstars.

"Aside from dogs, what's your favorite animal?"

"Goats. They jump off of rocks and make sassy noises. Alpacas are cool too, but awkward, which is why goats are number one."

"The alpacalypse!"

Around a plaster rock formation, the two of us marvel at a Komodo dragon.

"What's your animal fave?" she asks.

"You know this. Platypus. They use gravel for teeth. Their bills are electric. And they don't have nipples."

"Have you ever seen one in real life?"

"In America, we don't have Jaffa Cakes, and we don't have platypus."

After the zoo, we can't find a movie, so we watch cartoons on the couch with Gilligan. After it's over, in the doorway, I can't hug Annie long enough. Our perfect night is over where a year ago it would continue.

I drive the few blocks to my place. When your shoelaces freeze together, a Happiness Playlist is reason enough to stay in the van until they thaw. "Modern Girl" by Sleater-Kinney plays. I know this song is a satire, but it inspires me that artists are fighting oppressive systems with chords and lyrics.

Happiness is a fight to keep. I'm grateful for Sleater-Kinney.

Later, I wash the dishes. There are no clean towels, so I dry them with a shirt. When Dad was my age, he was married with two teenage boys and a house. I wonder if he dried dishes with a shirt.

The playlist has rewired my neural net. Since autumn, this is the most-listened-to song collection of my life. It's beyond familiar at this point. "You Turn Me On I'm a Radio" and "The Bare Necessities" are integrated into everything I do. The rhythm of my shower water taps out "Put on a Happy Face."

Come springtime, I'll be able to try the road again. To perform in cities a thousand miles away like I once did.

As a kid, the road took the form of Florida vacations, where Dad's dad took him on retreat. Orlando. Pensacola. West Palm Beach. Cocoa Beach. The tiny city of Stuart. A boy should be so lucky.

Once I began touring America with my music, the prospect of other states dawned on me as paradise as well. On an early tour I called Dad from the West Rim of the Grand Canyon.

"Hey, how come we went to Florida all those times and no place else? This is a most beautiful sight, Pops."

"Oh, yeah? Did you have a good time in Florida?"

"Of course."

"Then quit complaining, kid."

In Florida, we saw the Space Shuttle launch from the beach at dawn, where jellyfish washed up in polka dot patterns. Pirates of the Caribbean. Mom. Dad. Brother. Me. After college, my parents kept returning to Florida on vacations. My brother and I had moved away to different states.

I keep a photograph in a memento box under my bed. I found it when going through family albums for the lobby display at Mom's funeral. In it, she stands shrunken mid-frame. She's dwarfed by an empty winter beach and sea. Mom wears a thick coat. Her sunglasses are black orbs. Her mouth, expressionless, is straight across as the horizon behind her. This one wasn't included in her photo collage but I keep it as a tribute to her strength. It's a testimonial to her will against the darkness.

Mom said, "Mark, it pulls like a magnet."

On the morning of the fourth anniversary of her death, the city exhales. Wind batters the corner of my home. Sun soaks in through the lace diffusers. Bitter daylight glows. It is Sunday. I text Annie.

"Will you go to the church with me this afternoon? I'm scared to light candles by myself."

"Good morning. Sure. Why scared?"

"Confused."

"It'll be good. You'll feel better."

I stay under the blanket womb, gazing up till the ceiling disappears. I recall the night it happened. Dad's phone number rang, but it wasn't Dad. His friend said five words on the other end. "Mark, there's been an accident." Freezing rain stained and muted Minneapolis in a drab curtain. It choked me. My chest fluttered. I went numb.

Dad called twenty minutes later to confirm. He was crying.

"Mom died."

An asteroid hit the earth. Out the window, the planet's crust ripped open. An ice blue magma leapt into the streets. The city became a two-dimensional catastrophe zone. My jaw clenched. I'm surprised I didn't crush my own teeth. Reality was a shallow veil. Who prepares for this? One hundred razors cut my flesh into squares. They toppled over each other, squiggling on the hardwood. I didn't even notice.

In Wisconsin, a snowstorm was in full swing. My aunts told me not to drive until it blew over. They'd all come to the house to support Dad. I was assured he wouldn't be alone. By the time I got to the airport, the last plane for Milwaukee County had flown. My dear friend was willing to drive his truck, but it was too risky. We went back to the loft. There, I wailed a mournful howl of beasts. A cry from a beyond world. Never had a sound so raw come from inside me. Here was a soul disconnected from the body. A batholith of sorrow cracked the skull open sideways, releasing a solar system of tears to the apartment in one big bang. The universe contracted.

My kind uncle bought me a ticket for the next flight out at 6 a.m. From the air, a landscape of clouds stretched endlessly. Notions of heaven cooled my nausea. The natural artistry of airplane windows offered solace. I wondered if Mom was up there in some cloud I passed by. A jazz combo played on my earbuds. When the vibraphone came in, I released my pain. It soothed, the holy jazz. The tremolo of imagined bells pulled my senses together. An aunt and uncle met me when the plane landed. Nature unfolded through automatic actions of love. That we suffer alone is an illusion. They hugged me. We shared the pain. On the drive, I cried. In the driveway, I cried. In Dad's arms, we cried. It was a hard homecoming.

The loved ones came. They didn't knock, but they brought food. They brought open arms, consolation, and tears of their own. The organism of family bleeds and coagulates, adapts and evolves. Neighbors are family too. Father Jim said a prayer. Now I understand elephants, who mourn en masse.

When the house was empty, Dad, who never drinks, brought out brandy.

"Sometimes, we do this."

I'd never seen him do this. Dad isn't a man for the hard

stuff, but he poured out shots for both of us. We'd been awake for two days. Brandy was the sleep remedy. It was the one time I'd been drunk with my old man. We told stories until our words slurred. He went to bed singing Mom's name. I slept in the basement with earplugs in just like I still do now. It was the first night of abstract nightmares, the beginning of night running. Shadowy box shapes and screaming steel wheels. These lasted a year before becoming tangible dreams again.

My brother and his sweet family arrived the next day. Having a tiny nephew around lifted the room. Mom didn't make arrangements, so we went to the funeral home to pick out the urn. Pink with flowers. Looking back, I'm surprised we could even drive ourselves. There was an obituary to write and pictures to gather. Planning a funeral is a cruel necessity. We ordered floral arrangements. Dad was signing off on things and crying in between. The rising cost of dying loved is a disgusting number.

At the house, aunts rotated meals on the table. Lasagna. Ham sandwiches. They sometimes got loud with laughter, which, although it seemed inappropriate, was a break in the sadness. The funeral home called and asked for one of us to retrieve Mom's belongings delivered from the coroner's office. I went. They handed me a large zip sack with her wallet, keys, a watch, and gloves. My brain still has the details jumbled. On my drive, I kept the bag of items pressed into my chest under my coat. Tiny shreds of her energy hummed inside those belongings.

"Oh, Mommy." I cried gallons. "Why?"

Over the week that followed, the extended family emergency unit dispersed back to their own jobs and houses. Dad, my brother, and I came together without Mom. Now we'd need to lean on one another for support. She was in some other world of singing and dancing. She was with Elvis. She was with Patsy Cline. She was with Grandma, Grandpa, and Uncle Pat.

While cleaning up, I found a novel. *H.R.H.* by Danielle Steele. A page was folded. It felt still warm, still Mom. The marked moment became unfinished business. But also proof that she had full intention of finishing the book. Faith in the future. It put a cog in my head. If she didn't care anymore, why fold a page? Why bring her wallet?

"You'll never know why," said Father Kurt. "No matter how you debate and wonder in your head. It's between her and God."

"Will she go to hell?"

"No. Why would she?"

"Because that's what people say."

"Who? That was all changed in Vatican II. Your mother will go to heaven."

I didn't know about Vatican II. Did Mom? My fear is that anyone should live their last seconds thinking they're going anywhere other than someplace better. We picked out the songs to be sung at Mass. Father Kurt asked if I would be performing anything.

"'Let It Be,'" I said.

Four years on, the wound stays fresh. Old folks tell me I'll never get over it. They say it'll be easier to accept over time. Gratefulness is an efficient healing mechanism. This wisdom has been invaluable.

Annie texts.

"When would you like to go to the Basilica?"

"Now-ish?"

"Yes. That's fine."

We go. The side entrance to the Basilica of Saint Mary is a gold door. Its window is barred in thick iron. A statue of Saint John B. M. Vianney watches in a black cloak.

Inside, an organist is rehearsing for the 5 p.m. mass. Pipes echo off the granite church. Spears of colored light cut down at angles to the floor, catching the swirled dust like snowflakes. A young couple snaps selfies under the stations of the cross. On the walk to the votive candle rack, we pass a vivid stained-glass image of barefoot Moses. Underneath, it reads "Exodus XX:12 Honor thy father and thy mother."

At the Basilica of Saint Mary, a small votive costs a dollar; a large is five dollars. I splurge on the fiver. If there was a one-hundred-dollar candle, I'd buy that. I bet they got those at the Vatican.

Annie puts her hand on my shoulder as I kneel. "I'll be looking around."

Often, I've felt like the only person who ever lost their mother. It's not untrue to say death makes victims of us all. In front of me stands the virgin. Under a royal-blue robe, she wears a gold dress of elaborate tiles. Candles reflect in the flickering mosaic. Mary faces down and away in prayer. There are votive stations in all four corners of the Basilica. I cup my hands as Mary does. Tears fall before anything can be said. This swells to a silent sob.

"I love you, Mama," I whisper. "Thank you for the kisses, carousel rides, blueberry pancakes in animal shapes, state fair lights, welcome-back hugs, song advice, this soft heart, pianos, the raspberry milkshake when I broke my elbow, holding me even though I had the flu, teaching me to sing till we both cried, the goldfish on my birthday, laughing together in movies, laughing on the phone, laughing at the dog, laughing at the world, summer beach trips to Minooka Park, miniature golfing twice in one day, bowling lessons, and showing me to step-step-glide. If Mom love was money, I'd be a billionaire. Is that really you in dreams? Dad says so. He brought me one of your angels; she lives on my nightstand. I suppose you already know that. I wish I could call you. I'm sorry life became sad. I hope you are happy and safe now. Have you seen how big the nephews are getting? It's wonderful. If you can pull any strings where you are, make sure they're protected from bad stuff. Everybody misses you down here. Especially your sister. Especially Dad. Especially your two sons. I bet you're famous wherever you are. I wish Annie could meet you. I'm sorry I never got married. Can you see my concerts? Do you notice all the times I look into the light on stage? I'm looking at you, Mommy. I miss your voice. Thank you for teaching me kindness. After the funeral, I dreamed that you were a librarian. You told me to be soft, and to help people laugh so that they can shine. I asked you what softness means, and you said it's what we do when we are unconditional. Thank you for creating a gorgeous life for me. I know it was uphill for you. Have you asked God why? You deserve an answer. I love you, Mama. It's neat when you still show up in magical ways. I can't wait to see you again; there's so much more to say."

Four years earlier, on the blue light-rail line from the airport, my first encounter with the after-death happened. Offices and parking lots breezed by as the tracks bounced and rattled. In a snap, a surge went through me. There was an energy shift. It was a subtle, but definite change. Imagine switching the kitchen light out and the living room light on at the same time, while standing in the doorway between them. It was Mom. My identity of her, teleported from inside, to hovering on the top of my skin. A second skin. An aura. A telekinetic shell.

The second awakening came days later. I was roaming aimlessly about the North Loop. All I saw were shadows. Numbness surrounded. My hearing went dull. What was second nature two weeks earlier had become an uphill climb.

All my focus was concentrated to double-check traffic at stoplights. There were a number of near misses. It was effort to climb stairs. It was work to write an email or call a friend. How could I trust a world anymore? I built emotional muscles that I didn't know existed. The new normal was an exhausting adjustment.

Walking the streets, my thin jacket let the freeze in. I was indifferent to the weather. Like wearing earplugs, the sounds inside my body were louder than the sounds outside. Swallowing, exhaling, even footsteps roared over passing trucks. The sidewalks and skyline were faceless.

Mom was before anything. Before I knew of cities or trains. Before trees, clocks, or winter boots. Before music. Before I saw the sun. A smokestack leaned to one side. Behind it, the clean silhouettes of the skyscrapers downtown. They stood straight and tall, the smokestack slanted in the foreground. I cocked my head to match its angle. Minneapolis sliding perpetually off the earth. I'd found a totem. A name for the new way. The smokestack was my pivot point. With nothing to lean on, it persisted. If a thing of such industrial grandeur can stand, so could I.

Pink's song "Try" was released as a single in October 2012. I didn't hear it until March 2013. Pink's empowerment inspired Mom. I wonder if she ever heard Pink's lyrics to "Try"? They would have impressed her. When Pink played First Avenue on July 5, 2006, Mom and Dad drove up from Wisconsin. We watched from the owner's box. Mom beamed brighter than the spotlight at her hero. She sang along louder than the speaker system. When I hear "Try," it's as if sung to my mother. I hear a message of perseverance. When I hear "Try," I hear a message of acceptance. I hear healing.

Annie and I leave the Basilica and get our favorite pizza. Deep dish. Pineapple and green olive. I am linked to Annie and can't let go. Taking a Sunday afternoon to watch your ex-boyfriend light a votive at the Basilica isn't something of martyrs, but it means the world to me. The sadness fades with dinner. Annie and I joke about imagined pets and invented worlds. Down the block, Mom's five-dollar ballerina flame sways. My hope is that she is in her afterlife doing the same dance.

We are born by our dearest ancestors. Loved ones shape us with honesty, loyalty, positive morality, and gentle behavior. Gripping the zip-zap intelligence of boomerang kindness, we kiss the stars within our own newborn baby's hand. When the ever-flowing body stream explodes its molten core, hundreds of millions of tears bound out. The physical self collapses under the super continent of the soul.

Dad calls. I tell him about the votive. He says he's certain Mom is watching over us. Then we speak of snowstorms. In the fifties he had sledded on waxed cardboard down the hill behind the tennis courts of North Lincoln Memorial Drive. That's off the shoreline of Lake Michigan. Though they fight to break free by darting and stabbing and pulling toward the sky, it's the string that binds them and keeps kites flying.

Spring

The speaker on my music player is lit but nothing plays. The volume is down. I walk over to it. Instead of turning it up, I power it down. I don't even look on the screen to see what song is playing. I feel confidence. The Happiness Playlist is inside me now. At least it'd better be; I'd listened to Pharrell's "Happy" over a hundred times that winter. Feel-good music doesn't fail me. Major chords and positive lyrics give faith to know that everything works out all right. Continued therapy and my positive support system assist in the heavy lifting. Time passing helps too. Then again, maybe it is all Mom, pulling strings from the beyond. However things work, I can say with great confidence that happy music unsticks the muck from the boot heels.

Annie texts.

"It's nice out!"

"Yes! There was a doggo at Walgreen's today. When I called it a good dog, it looked away."

"I wonder why. Was it actually a bad dog?"

"I guess so."

"Maybe you caused it to realize it has the potential to be a good dog someday."

"True." I reply. "If you're called bad dog your whole life, you don't know any different."

"Until one day this cool dude comes along and calls you a good dog."

"You think it thought I was cool?"

"Heck yeah, you're cool."

"You're cool too, Annie."

More time goes by in another green/gray world. At night, I play a solo concert in a basement. During the day, the sun blazes, but it is still too early for air conditioners. I stand naked in the kitchen, drinking my tea from a mug that reads "I am Wonder Woman." Frozen mini tacos thaw in the microwave.

Dad calls.

"These things are bad news. I'm going to get a taco belly."

"If you don't want them, don't eat them."

"But they're great!"

"Don't put a negative spin on everything. Just enjoy the tacos."

"You're right, Dad. Oh hey, something weird happened at the solo show I played last night."

"Yeah?"

"It was a benefit event in some hip agency." I say. "I was playing on a tiny stage used otherwise for corporate presentations. Toward the end of the set, I talked about Mom. Between songs, I said that it's been difficult to accept how she died. I also said that I missed her. Then a digital static burst over the PA speakers. A voice sound cracked in short spurts. It went on for about five seconds. I said, 'Mom? Is that you?' into the microphone. The crowd laughed, sort of, and I started the next song. Afterward, I asked this guy if he heard the static interruption. He said the whole place heard it, and how could they not? I think it was her."

"Definitely. It was."

On Memorial Day, I sit by the creek alone. It's the same spot Annie and I come for summer picnics. On the parkway, motorcycles roam amid church bell anthems at noon. Laughing teenagers fall from trees. After four feverish months, the drugstore has restocked its cough drops. The last snow piles are found only in parking lots. Runaway shopping carts, how did you get so far?

In the gardens off Lake Harriet, a wood post reads "May peace prevail on earth." There is a fence around the roses. Questionable hammocks swing between trees and giggle.

It is a still sunset, the kind where you go outside in a sleeveless shirt and no jacket. There are June bugs. They fly into the side of the house with a smack and also into my hair. I shriek. They land on the driveway and flip upside down. I help a stuck one get right side up. It flies away, a shot helicopter.

Then come days of wondering. If the universe is not made of atoms, could it be made of cookies? Asteroid belts of moon-sized cookies, smashing against one another in chaotic jest. We're absorbed in mathematics and sensibility; meanwhile, our brain lacks the capacity to understand itself. We quarrel over worthless crumbs, entrapped in a circle of pointed fingers. We bicker. We wonder. We never know.

But there are loopholes. For instance, music. Imagine all the songs ever sung, joined together into one sublime tone. Something beyond words, beyond judgment. How would it sound? All coming together in a perfect, simple note. Hear it with the inner ear, resonating. Now sing it to life. Feel it pass the throat and lips into the air. Let it vibrate into the world. The root of all music is right there inside of us all along. Music is not the mouth that is singing. It's the heart.

Music is a story. In the best stories, a couple falls in love, and nothing goes wrong. A line worker wins the lottery, buys the factory, and turns it into an amusement park. A dwarf meets ten aardvarks and they all live together in a treehouse. There are no bad guys. Nobody gets hurt. The music never ends.

Then Annie texts. She is flustered.

"Mark! Gilligan was digging by the fence when I heard squeaking. I'm pretty sure it was a baby bunny. The thorn bushes made it hard to see if he got anything. He wouldn't come back inside. I had to pick him up. I'm afraid to go look."

"Want me to?"

"Yes."

I drive over. She is in the kitchen, holding the dog. Gilligan pants with excitement and struggles in her grasp. One often hears stories of a pet who catches an animal, then doesn't know what do next.

"He wasn't being bad," she says. "He didn't know better."

Gilligan makes the confused face of domesticated inner turmoil. Picture two people trapped in an elevator. A day goes by. Eventually, primal instinct takes over. They tear each other's clothes off and do the deed. Then the elevator gets unstuck. News cameras flash as the doors open to reveal a mad swirl of intertwined flesh. Spouses gasp. Imagine the faces on the two trapped passengers, torn from desperate lust. Shock. Embarrassment. This is the same face on Annie's dog. Wide eyed. Mouth open. Eyeballs averted.

She follows me into the yard. The dog stays inside. Lush grass is overgrown. It slows the feet in a comfortable way.

"Oh my god! There it is!" Annie whispers in terror.

The bunny lies still, cradled by the tall green lawn. Its back legs are twisted and spread sideways. The eyes are clear and unmoving. I lean over it and see a rapid flutter of breath. My hand strokes the rabbit's fur. There is warmth.

"It's not dead," I say. The bunny is smooth underneath.

Its little heart throbs in my cupped palm.

Annie hurries inside and comes back with a shoe box. We fill it with a bed of soft grass. The rabbit doesn't blink.

"It must be in shock."

I call the Minnesota Wildlife Rehabilitation Center. They close at 8 p.m. It is 7:35. I need to speed on the freeway, but it's possible to get there before it closes. We jump into the van.

Annie peers in the box as we get on the expressway. "She's curled up in the corner."

"Thankfully, old Gilligan doesn't have many teeth left," I say, whipping through traffic.

My 3.6-liter V6 gets us into the rehab center parking lot at 7:55 p.m. We run into the building. The waiting room has those same fabric and wood task chairs you see in hospitals. With great relief, we pass the shoebox to the woman over the counter.

"What have we got?" she says.

"A baby rabbit," I reply. "It was in the dog's mouth."

The woman hands us a form on a clipboard. The bunny in the box is taken away. Annie breathes a heavy sigh. On the wall is a list of animals rehabilitated back into the wild. American Robins 247. Wood Ducks 287. Mallard Ducks 643. Eastern Grey Squirrels 1,051. Eastern Cottontail is the highest. 2,505. Now 2,506.

"The rabbit will be assessed by the vet. If there's no injury, it goes into our nursery. If there is an injury, they'll determine whether they can treat it. If there is an injury and it cannot be treated, they will humanely euthanize it so it doesn't suffer."

"You've seen a lot of stuff; do you think that bunny will be OK?" I ask.

"It's temperament seemed good. If you don't see external injuries, there's still the chance of internal, but they'll check things out thoroughly."

"Will it go in the refuge afterward?"

"We do releases all around the metro. Sometimes we take them out to rural areas and let them go."

"Thank you for helping us." Annie hands her the paperwork.

"I'm glad you made it in time," the woman replies.

I buy a decorative plate for a small donation. It shows a forest scene with cartoon owls, rabbits, and squirrels playing in the snow. The money is a donation, but I think of it as a bribe. It's after closing time. Instead of going back to the van, we walk into the wildlife refuge. A wide gravel path leads onto a wooden walkway through a marsh. Purple wildflowers and tall swamp grasses decorate either side. The sky is tangerine and the sun has already disappeared. Lining the walkway is knee-high fencing on worn wood posts.

"Good thing you went out and checked on Gilligan," I say.

"He was in the yard for a few minutes when I heard the squeaking. That's when I ran outside. He wouldn't leave the thorn bushes. I had to pull him by the leg."

"Could the bunny have hopped out from the bushes afterward?"

"He could have chomped or just pawed it. I don't know."

Birds chirp. There is no movement to the air. The evening glistens. All of fresh spring is settling in as if dreary winter was an urban myth. A Dad joke.

"I know the squeak. I know it because I've been around a dog that did get two baby bunnies. It was the same scared squeak."

"She was docile when I picked her up. I bet she's a survivor," I say. "I hope they release her out here in the refuge."

"It's pretty."

In fifteen minutes, the whole wetland becomes a silhou-
ette. Shadows gather the inverse of day. It is too dark to see
anymore. We turn around. All life is entangled in shades of
monochrome blue.

In loving memory of Lila Mallman (1945–2013)

Acknowledgments

Everything in this book happened. I changed the names of people. Some were combined. A street name or two got adjusted. Some little stuff happened in a different order but mostly the guts of the story are the way it went down. All of it is real. Especially the part about happiness.

Here's where I say thank you but it's not enough. Words can tell a story but they can't approximate my gratitude to those who enabled this book's creation. Now I know what people mean in speeches when they say they apologize in advance to anyone they may have left out.

Thank you to my father. The bowling pin lamp you made for me will never be shut off. Thank you for showing me how to work hard, enjoy life, eat bakery, pet dogs—and for buying the piano. I can hear you in my head right now saying, "Hour by hour, day by day, getting better in every way." You're the wisest philosopher I ever met. I love you and can't wait to hug you again. Thank you, Brian, for setting the highest standards of kindness. Remember the time we drove to House on the Rock together? That was one of my life top 100. My god, how can one man be supportive of so much positivity? Thank you for helping the homeless. Thank you for bringing musicians together all across the porches of earth. I'm in awe of your heart. You also have beautiful line quality. I love you.

Thank you to Blake Iverson for your steadfast dedication to my vision, bold honesty, and over a decade of legal witchcraft. Thank you, Adam Wahlberg, for taking the leap. We landed safe without parachutes. What started over pizza has now become a full-grown, beautiful Frankenstein of feel-great vibes. It's pretty damn neat, buddy. Thank you, Ryan Scheife, for your dazzling design upon these pages, and for playing bass on *The Tourist* in 1997. Thank you, Lauren Wuornos, for going into the mud and rain to make some fun art and stumbling into a book cover with me. Also, for buying my movie tickets. I owe you. Thank you, Katie Sisneros, Sarah Wefald, Paul Dickinson, Holly Day, Anne Conklin, David Toht, Carolyn Swiszcz, and Adrian Todd Zuniga for your notes, your patience, and for guiding my words. They wouldn't be in the right order without you. I love you.

Thank you, Wilson Webb, for your artful eye and for living in my heart every moment. It's been a lot of pizzas. Someday we will watch our movie together, and hopefully not under The Tree. You were an exemplary human when we met in the '90s. You were an exemplary human when I got sick. You are an exemplary human now. I love you. Thank you, Troy Schaefer, for being there when I called you. I'm glad we didn't brave the blizzard that night, but I'm forever grateful you offered. RIP, Big Block. Some of the best nights though, damn. You taught/teach me how to let life lead. I love you. Thank you, Ben Conrad, for ghosts and projects. I'm glad we have our Sunday talks. I'm also glad you don't drink vodka out of a mug anymore. Success doesn't have a ceiling for you. You're a superhero to me. I love you. Thank you, Dan Geller, for music and science. Ruby forever! Thanks for all the nights out dancing. You even laugh at my worst jokes. I guess that's one of many reasons everybody thinks you're magic. I love you. Thank you Mary and the boys. I love you lots lots lots. Thank you, B, for getting me through it. Thank you for showing me how to love animals on a deeper level. Thank you for these words: "You got this. You made it through last time; you can do it again." Thank you for silliness, as potent as poison but the other way around. Thank you for G. Thank you for Owly and The Scarecrows. Thank you for letting me cry in the flower garden. Thank you for not leaving me at my weakest. Thank you for teaching me the strength in being gentle. Thank you for shining.

Thank you, Aaron Lemay, for over a decade of U.S. tours. We've seen more madness and beauty than Han Solo and Chewbacca combined. (I can't decide which one of us is which, though.) There have been some pretty seedy dive bars along the way, and you've always shown me the door to a happiness—sometimes a pool table. Sonya was right when she called you a Bodhisattva. Also, thank you for giving me the hotel bed because I'm "older." I love you. Thank you, Scott McVeigh, Mike Geronsin, August Ogren, Peter Anderson, Ryan Plewacki, Vonnie Kyle, Ryan Smith, Kathie Pony Hixon-Smith, Jeremy Ylvisaker, Bill Shaw, Ryan Olson, Chris Rosenau, Sean Hoffman, Matt Johnson, Craig Grossman, Charles Gehr, Sheila Kenny, Tyler Spencer, Chuck Prophet, Dylan Magierek, Darin Spring, Stephen Somers, John Foderick, Jacques Wait, Ed Ackerson, Brad Cassetto, Big Dog Anderson, Graham Elliot, Ian Rans, Hillary Churchill, Keith Moran, Dirt, Jim Weber, Mo Bluntz, Jillian Rae, Mark Fox, Nelson Devereaux, Brian Oake, Katrina Stubson, Matt Kruse, Kim Randall, Dan Didier, Sam Thompson, Caitlin Rae, Simon Calder, Katharine Seggerman, Everyone at In The Groove, Liz Draper, Ryan Olcott, Steve Seel, Sean Anonymous, Anna Gedstad, Sonia Grover, Nate Kranz, James

Buckley, Dave Weigert, Mary Lucia, Eric Parker Anderson, Aaron Poochigian, Anne Saxton, Kim Bartmann, Adam Toht, Barb Abney, Wendy Lynn Staats, Jason Nagel, and all the music folks who've made my career possible thus far. Thank you, Purple Banana, for telling me to live in my heart.

Thank you, Steve Marsh, for being enamored by life and spreading it like Nutella on toast. You're a hero, Stephen. Aim for the heart of the hole. Thank you, Erin Muir, for opera and pancakes and understanding why *Grease 2* is magic. You are magic too, but in a different way. Thank you, Stuart Devaan, for robots and connectivity (of the heart and otherwise). Thank you, Alice, for the world's best peanut butter cookies, keeping book love alive, believing in ghosts, and ultimately your glowing spirit of loving kindness. Thank you, First Avenue, for being a home to my music since the early days. I want to kiss every one of your black bricks until the city quarantines me. I got my bachelor's degree in art school but I got my PhD at First Avenue. Without you, my life would be profoundly different.

Before and after it all, there is Minneapolis. Thank you for the music. Thank you for embracing diversity and open-mindedness. Thank you for supporting the arts. Thank you for speaking against hate. Thank you for summer festivals and winter fantastics. Thank you for singing along. Thank you for loving me. I love you too, Minneapolis.

Mark Mallman is a songwriter, composer, and performer from Minneapolis. He has recorded eight albums and his music has been enjoyed by audiences worldwide. His non-stop, non-sleep, "Marathon III" performance stretched 78 hours and included 576 pages of rhyming lyrics. Mallman's album "The End is Not The End" is a deliberate meditation on overcoming the roots of despair. He was born in Milwaukee.

The Happiness Playlist

1. "And It Stoned Me" —Van Morrison
2. "The Bare Necessities" —Phil Harris & Bruce Reitherman
3. "By Your Side" —Sade
4. "California Stars" —Billy Bragg and Wilco
5. "Can I Kick It?" —A Tribe Called Quest
6. "Cool Jerk" —The Capitols
7. "Dance to the Music" —Sly & The Family Stone
8. "Digital Witness" —St. Vincent
9. "Ease on Down the Road" —Diana Ross & Michael Jackson
10. "Escapade" —Janet Jackson
11. "Everybody Eats When They Come to My House" —Cab Calloway
12. "Fantasy" —Mariah Carey
13. "Fields of Gold" —Sting
14. "For Once in My Life" —Stevie Wonder
15. "Friendship" —Pops Staples
16. "Genesis" —Grimes
17. "Good As Hell" —Lizzo
18. "Good Times" —The Persuasions
19. "Happy" —Pharrell Williams
20. "Hot Topic" —Le Tigre
21. "I Got You (I Feel Good)" —James Brown & The Famous Flames
22. "I'll Take You There" —The Staple Singers
23. "I Love Music" —The O'Jays
24. "Imagine" —John Lennon
25. "I Wanna Dance With Somebody (Who Loves Me)" —Whitney Houston

Your Happiness Playlist

1.
2.
3.
4.
5.
6.
7.
8.
9.
10.
11.
12.
13.
14.
15.
16.
17.
18.
19.
20.
21.
22.
23.
24.
25.

26.

27.

28.

29.

30.

31.

32.

33.

34.

35.

36.

37.

38.

39.

40.

41.

42.

43.

44.

45.

46.

47.

48.

49.

50.